D1519772

ARTISTS OF THE HARLEM RENAISSANCE

JAMES VAN DER ZEE

PHOTOGRAPHER

LARA ANTAL

Cavendish
Square

New York

Published in 2017 by Cavendish Square Publishing, LLC
243 5th Avenue, Suite 136, New York, NY 10016

Library of Congress Cataloging-in-Publication Data

Antal, Lara, author.
James Van Der Zee / Lara Antal.
pages cm. — (Artists of the Harlem Renaissance)
Includes bibliographical references and index.
ISBN 978-1-5026-1066-9 (hardcover) ISBN 978-1-5026-1067-6 (ebook)
1. Van Der Zee, James, 1886-1983. 2. Photographers—United States—Biography. 3. African American photographers—New York (State)—New York—Biography. 4. Harlem Renaissance.
I. Van Der Zee, James, 1886-1983, photographer. II. Title.
TR140.V37A58 2016
770.92—dc23
[B]
2015036565

Editorial Director: David McNamara
Editors: Amy Hayes/Kristen Susienka
Copy Editor: Nathan Heidelberger
Art Director: Jeffrey Talbot
Designer: Stephanie Flecha
Production Assistant: Karol Szymczuk
Photo Research: J8 Media

Printed in the United States of America

TABLE OF CONTENTS

PART 1

The Life of James Van Der Zee

"Happiness is like perfume, you can't pour it on somebody else without getting a few drops on yourself."

—James Van Der Zee

Opposite: James Van Der Zee at Homestead, circa 1900.

CHAPTER ONE

THE EARLY YEARS

James Van Der Zee was one of the greatest photographers of the Harlem Renaissance. What makes his story so incredible is that neither he nor the public at large would know this until much later in his life.

THE VAN DER ZEE FAMILY

James Augustus Joseph Van Der Zee was born on June 19, 1886. The second oldest in a family of six children, Van Der Zee was born into a supportive and loving household. His father and mother were encouraging and hardworking individuals. Jennie Van Der Zee, the eldest child, was born in 1885, followed by James, Walter, Charles, Johnny, and then Mary. Johnny died of pneumonia at the age of six and James would only remember him vaguely. Despite this tragedy, the Van Der Zees' family bonds stayed strong. It was during his childhood years that James developed a love of the arts and a deep respect for his fellow man.

Opposite: The Van Der Zee Homestead

Originally from New York City, Van Der Zee's parents, John and Susan Van Der Zee, had served as butler and maid in the home of Ulysses S. Grant, Civil War general and later the president of the United States. Unfortunately, Susan became pregnant with their first child right before the Grant fortune fell way to debtors, and so the Van Der Zees decided to leave New York City in 1884 to raise their family in the small town of Lenox, Massachusetts.

Formerly a writers' colony, then a failed industrial town, Lenox had become a summer home for many of New England's wealthiest families. The Vanderbilts, Westinghouses, and Morgans, among others, had come to call Lenox home for the warmer seasons. Lenox's economy was all but entirely fueled by businesses that catered to wealthy vacationers. In the summer seasons, the town swelled by the hundreds and in the off seasons, it shrank to only eight hundred or nine hundred residents.

The Van Der Zees were one of a half dozen black families in the area. Once they arrived in Lenox, their neighborhood became populated with relatives. Eventually, all three generations of Van Der Zees lived alongside one another on Tatonic Street. First, John and Susan Van Der Zee moved in. Then, David and Josephine Osterhout, James's grandparents, and their four daughters moved in beside them. Finally, the last residence was home to James's great-aunts, Fanny and Lena Egbert. James remembered the family acreage fondly: "We were all together, three little houses together. There was my aunts' house, our house, and my grandparents' house. We had a stable and my grandparents had a stable, and they had a henhouse and we had a henhouse."

For many years, his extended family lived comfortably in Lenox. His grandmother operated a laundry service, the Egbert sisters ran a bakery, and his mother cooked and cared for her growing family. John Van Der Zee, in addition to maintaining the homestead and family farm, worked at the local Episcopalian church. Supported in part by the wealthy summer visitors, the Trinity Church had hired John to serve as their **sexton**, or groundskeeper. This, along with odd jobs around town, provided the family with a steady income throughout most of their time in Lenox. There was always plenty of food on the table, and the Van Der Zees faced little economic hardship or family strife. Biographer Jim Haskins put it best: "It was a happy household, a simple life that revolved around hard work and the church, good food and simple pleasures." The family flourished under these fortunate conditions.

While in Lenox, James Van Der Zee and his siblings attended a public school that taught both white and black students. His classmates were predominantly white; he and his siblings would often be the only black children in class. Van Der Zee never recalled encountering any discrimination, partly because his interactions were limited to formal settings such as school and church. While Lenox proved to be a "relatively benign environment for blacks," Van Der Zee does recall being regarded with a "certain feeling of inferiority," partly due to the lack of understanding from his other classmates: "We knew we looked different from the others, and a lot of the kids didn't understand that we weren't black by choice."

Van Der Zee did not like school much. He disliked the tedium of studying and felt it took "too much brain work." However, he took to anything that could spark his imagination. In this way, he loved reading stories and poetry:

> I was so anxious to read that I learned early. My aunts used to tell us stories, as the twilight came on, about [Native Americans], and we would imagine we saw their camp fires burning … I had a great many favorite poems, mostly ones that were descriptive. Some of the poems would put pictures in your mind and you could practically see a picture.

A CREATIVE SPARK

An imaginative child, Van Der Zee loved to express himself in creative ways. His entire family was creative: John Van Der Zee taught his children to paint, his aunts sang in a quartet, and his grandmother and great-aunts played the fiddle and guitar. During long winter hours, the family would draw and paint together to pass time.

Both James and his older sister Jennie exhibited natural talents for the arts. Jennie was a superb musician and painter. She often played the organ at church; it was joked that she would play even before her legs could reach the pedals. James, too, was a talented musician and taught himself to play the piano and violin. As a painter, he felt he was "most successful at landscapes," but could never get faces to look right. It was this "shortcoming" that helped spark his interest in photography: "After I found out there was such a thing as a camera and that you could put people in position and just press the button and you had the picture, then I didn't do so much drawing and painting."

INTRODUCING THE CAMERA

One day, Van Der Zee saw an ad in a magazine called *Youth's Companion*. This ad said if you could sell twenty packets of ladies' sachet at ten cents each, they would send you a small camera outfit. Van Der Zee immediately wrote to the company and began selling to everyone and anyone he knew. It took him over two months—partly because there were so few potential customers that he had to wait until his first customers ran out of their supply. However, in the end, Van Der Zee earned the full amount and mailed it back. He had won his prize:

> One day there was a little red card indicating that there was a package too big to go in the mailbox. My blood pressure must have run up to about 290, I guess, until the man found the package and brought it out. It was about the size of four cough drop boxes all together, and in it there were two or three packages—envelopes of chemicals, a developer and clearing solution, and a small box of 2.5 × 2.5 inch [6.35 by 6.35 centimeter] plates.

Van Der Zee and brother Walter snowshoeing, circa 1900.

Van Der Zee was never able to produce any real images with this small camera. At one point, he saw a scratch on the plate and thought it was the beginning of an image, but when he brought it out into the light the plate had turned entirely black. While his prize proved to be anticlimactic, he was not discouraged. He memorized the camera and developing instructions and set out to find better photographic equipment. His curiosity had been piqued.

EARNING HIS KEEP

In order to save up a little money, James and his brother Walter began working for one of the summer residents, Mrs. David Dana. She had a big garden that needed tending and offered them twenty-five cents an hour to pull weeds and plant flowers.

A RENAISSANCE MAN IN THE HARLEM RENAISSANCE

Actor Vincent Price said, "A man who limits his interests limits his life." James Van Der Zee was the furthest possible from this; he was both a master photographer and an accomplished musician. Van Der Zee had considered a music career for most of his young life. In New York City, he joined the Amsterdam Musical Association, the Clef Club, and took courses at the Cogden Conservatory of Music. He frequently played at dance schools, churches, and other social functions. He worked at his sister's school, the Toussaint Conservatory of Art and Music, teaching violin lessons. By 1913, he was listed in the city directory as a musician. The following year, he formed a five-piece band called the Harlem Orchestra and played events around the city. When his photography business first started, Van Der Zee frequently took gigs at night and on weekends. He played accompaniment music to silent films at the Lincoln Theater and performed in the pit for live shows at the Lafayette Theatre in Harlem. His last professional performance was with Fletcher Henderson, an important big band jazz leader and musical arranger. Music had always been Van Der Zee's passion, but with new technologies, especially records, it became difficult to make a living off it. About records, Van Der Zee said, "You could hear yourself playing, but you didn't get paid." To support his family, Van Der Zee turned to photography. However, music would always remain his first love.

Once James had earned five dollars he sent away for his next camera. Purchased through mail order from a company in New York City, this camera proved to be much sturdier. A 4-by-5-inch (10.2 by 12.7 cm) Klieg camera, it had to be operated on a stand. It used glass plates, and since there were no local shops that could develop these, nor could he send them away, Van Der Zee learned to process his own plates.

By then he was in the fifth grade and had begun taking photos of his classmates for practice. One day, the teacher saw him and asked how much each of the photos cost. Van Der Zee replied, "Oh, ten cents apiece," and she began to list off an order: six of these, eight of these, etc. Van Der Zee was so ashamed to take the money that he ended up not finishing the photos. At the time, he had no idea that "people made a living taking pictures." He was just enthused about his new hobby.

But Van Der Zee wasn't the only one excited; his family enjoyed seeing his photographs and encouraged him to keep making them. Van Der Zee had his own bedroom, and no one objected when he turned his closet into a darkroom: "You didn't need much for a darkroom in those days," said Van Der Zee, "just some chemicals and three trays and a darkroom light. We didn't have electricity then, so my light was a candle inside a collapsible metal enclosure with one side that was red glass. You'd have to put the prints out in the sunlight after treating them."

Van Der Zee photographed many of Lenox's wealthy summer residents, including the Vanderbilts, Morgans, Westingtons, Frelinghuysens, the Lemeers, and the Parsons. In fact, some of these photos would come back to him in surprising ways as an adult. Once, years later, when he owned his own studio in Harlem, a group of young people stopped by to have their photos taken. They were on their way to the doctor and thought, since one of the boys was headed into the Air Force, this would be a good opportunity to have pictures made. Jokingly, Van Der Zee asked if they could take his wife for a joyride in an airplane.

They entertained the idea and asked where she wanted to go. Van Der Zee replied, "Not very far, only out to my home in Lenox, Massachusetts." This struck a chord with one of the girls:

> She mentioned one family, and I went to the drawer ... and pulled out a letter that was addressed to me from the Hotel Eden in Rome, Italy. The letter said that it was very sweet of me to send those lovely photographs and that I deserved a great deal of credit for taking such good pictures ... As the girl was reading the letter, she was amazed to find that it was from her mother—because I had made the pictures for her mother before she—the daughter—was ever born ... She was shocked and surprised at the coincidence that she could drop into this little dump, in Harlem, and find letters from her mother.

The girl begged for a copy of the letter because her mother had died. Van Der Zee gladly provided it and the group purchased over fifty dollars' worth of photos. A few weeks later, Van Der Zee saw in the Sunday section of the *Journal American* that the mysterious girl was married to one of Andrew Carnegie's sons.

Around age twelve or fourteen, Van Der Zee decided to quit school in order to start earning money. From a young age, he and his siblings had helped their father with work at Trinity Church: polishing brass, dusting pews, mowing lawns, even helping him dig graves. Unfortunately, the years as sexton had been physically hard on John Van Der Zee. He was diagnosed with tuberculosis, a possible result from years of carrying and inhaling ashes from the church's furnace. In 1902, he left his job at Trinity to work as a waiter at the newest vacationer hotel, the Aspinwall. Van Der Zee had been working odd jobs around town and decided to follow his father to the Aspinwall. However, the position was especially short lived, for Van Der Zee's father soon decided to go to New York City to look for work.

Van Der Zee would always consider this the time when the family "broke up." His father left for the big city while Van Der Zee continued to work at the Aspinwall. He stayed there until, one day, he was fired for a misunderstanding:

> The headwaiter said he'd heard I'd broken a whole tray full of dishes. I said I had only broken one—a dish with a cover on it. There was a Greek dishwasher there and he said I'd broken a whole trayful. Well, he had a very inviting nose and he was standing a little *too close* to me, I popped him one … and lost the job on that account … I never went too much for fighting, but I was quick-tempered then.

After this incident, Van Der Zee had a hard time finding work in the small town of Lenox. Around early 1905, he and his brother Walter decided to leave their hometown and join their father in New York City.

WELCOME TO HARLEM

When the Van Der Zees arrived in New York City, Harlem was beginning to change. Originally coined "Haarlem," a Dutch name, this term was used to vaguely refer to most of upper Manhattan. By 1900 it had solidified to mean an area bounded by 110th Street on the south, 159th Street on the north, the East River, and present-day Morningside and St. Nicolas Avenues. Harlem had always been a residential neighborhood, initially home to many middle- and upper-class white New Yorkers. At the turn of the century, three of the elevated train lines were extended through Harlem to the Bronx, making Harlem even more accessible. With this new boom in interest, developers moved in and built apartments, brownstones, and town houses. However, their construction had gone too fast too soon, and by 1905, many of the homes stood empty. Desperate to recoup their losses, realtors turned to the newly emerging black middle class to fill these brand new homes at lower rates. Many of the black residents of New York City lived in San Juan Hill or the Tenderloin, both overcrowded, slum-ridden neighborhoods. Harlem had become a new frontier of opportunity.

The Van Der Zees did not initially live in Harlem, but in the more dangerous Tenderloin. The term "Tenderloin" was not unique to New York City: many cities had Tenderloin neighborhoods, marked by high crime rates. In New York City, this neighborhood was located much farther south than Harlem, running from 20th to 53rd Street, between Eighth and Ninth Avenues. Scattered across these blocks were enclaves of black communities, something Van Der Zee had never seen or experienced before in his predominantly white hometown of Lenox. To add further cultural shock, Van Der Zee was transitioning from being a country boy to a city dweller. From the cabs and trolleys to the storefronts and clubs to the theaters and public entertainments, Van Der Zee was both overwhelmed and intrigued: "It was very exciting. There were so many opportunities. And what I liked most about New York was that no matter what you were interested in, you could always find somebody better and there was no limit to how far you could go in any line you might be interested in."

Van Der Zee began working odd jobs around the city as a waiter or elevator operator. These were the types of positions most readily accessible to black workers. Other positions, such as a cashier or a bank teller, were often posted as for "whites only." Van Der Zee noted these positions were off limits and not worth applying to: "They'd give you a long paper to fill out, and if you filled it out they'd think you were crazy. Call a paddy wagon! I wasn't going to be any trailblazer."

During this time, Van Der Zee tried a little bit of everything, not sticking to any one job or experience for too long. He worked for various employers, shot photography for friends and acquaintances, played violin, and sought out New York City

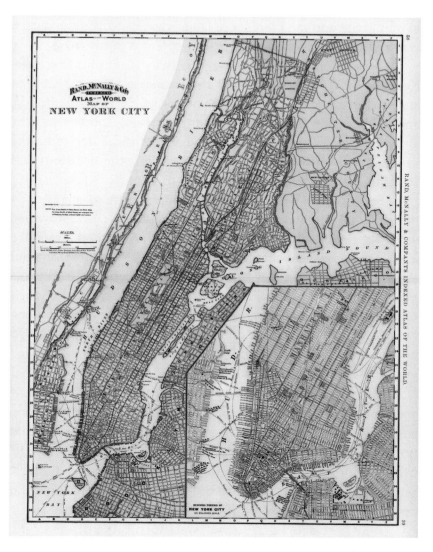

Map of New York City, circa 1893, with a closeup of lower Manhattan. The Tenderloin and Juan Hill neighborhoods were situated south of Central Park, while Harlem would emerge north of the park.

entertainments such as clubs and musical shows. Jazz was rising in popularity, and Van Der Zee, a fan of classical waltzes and rags, was still able to take on more paid work as a musician.

It was through one of these jobs that he met his first wife, Kate Brown. Van Der Zee played a violin solo at St. Mark's Church and Kate approached him after the performance. Young, fun-loving, and stubborn, Van Der Zee found her personality, Southern charm, and looks very attractive. He would always recall her as having "a mind of her own; she was good at making the decisions and so forth. I had no experience along those lines."

The young Van Der Zee had not planned on marrying until he had saved up some money, at least five hundred dollars. However, when Kate suddenly declared, "I believe you ruined me," Van Der Zee knew his plans would have to change. Kate was pregnant and Van Der Zee felt the only honorable thing to do was marry her. He recalled, "Since it was my child, why, then I'd be man enough to stand by it. When she said, 'No, I don't believe people get along well marrying under those circumstances,' she said that she'd go on about her business, and forget about it. Finally, I talked her into it." They were married in March 1907.

Afterward, the newly wed couple moved into their first apartment on West 29th Street. At first they had a hard time adjusting to their new financial independence; Van Der Zee did not foresee the expenses associated with starting a household. Everything from rent to furniture to moving caused them financial stress. Because of this, much to the Van Der Zee family's joy, the couple decided to move back to Lenox to have their child.

Their first daughter, Rachel, was born on September 22, 1907. Shortly after Rachel's birth, however, Kate wanted to visit her relatives down south. So, just as quickly as they had arrived in Lenox, the newly fledged family packed up and headed to Phoebus, Virginia.

Kate and Rachel, circa 1908.

DEVELOPING THE ARTIST

Throughout all his experiences, Van Der Zee kept up his photography as a casual hobby. However, it was during this period he would start to develop into an artist with real vision.

The photos Van Der Zee would take in Phoebus, Virgina, would be some of his first compelling images of the black community.

While in Virginia, Van Der Zee supported his family through hotel waiter jobs. However, much of his free time was spent at the Whittier School, a preparatory school for the all-black Hampton Institute in Hampton. This university, which had been established in 1868 to educate former slaves, had become a respected trade school by 1900. Van Der Zee enrolled in music courses there and, to his surprise, deeply impressed his classmates and professors. He became a minor celebrity around campus and performed at many local benefits and recitals.

His peers appreciated not only his music skills but his photography skills as well. He became the resident expert in the field and photographed many of his neighbors and friends. Van Der Zee possessed a sensitive command of light and texture and, through careful compositions, used these elements to create visual drama. The photos looked as if they were the work of a devotee of Renaissance paintings. However, to twenty-one-year-old Van Der Zee, they were simple expressions of sentiment. He earnestly described the inspiration for one of his famous photographs: "A couple of colored fellows had a blacksmith shop down there. Reminded me of a poem I learned in school, 'The Village Black Smith: Under the spreading chestnut tree the village smithy stands …' Music and art, they all seemed to work in conjunction, to my way of thinking."

While Van Der Zee enjoyed his time in Phoebus, he was anxious to return to New York. He did not like the segregation he experienced in the South; white and black people were separated on trains and other forms of public transportation. He had never experienced this before and felt it was distasteful. In addition, his creative respite at the Whittier School had sparked his confidence. He felt if he returned to the city he could make a decent living as a musician and better pursue his art. And so, quite resolved to return north, the young family headed back to New York City in spring of 1908.

Whittier Preparatory School class #2, circa 1906.

Whittier Preparatory School class #2, circa 1908.

CHAPTER TWO

DISCOVERING HARLEM

For many aspiring New Yorkers, Harlem promised a decent living. Thousands flocked to the neighborhood, including the Van Der Zees. Their apartment was at 138th Street and Lenox Avenue. In 1908, Kate was pregnant with their second child and the family had begun making financial preparations. Van Der Zee worked as an elevator operator for various buildings, played music gigs, and taught private lessons, while Kate took on sewing jobs. At one point, Van Der Zee even started selling shirts to make a little extra cash; he would purchase them wholesale and resell them on the street. He juggled many jobs at a time, but never for too long. This lifestyle paid the bills and, as he recalls it, he never went hungry.

FACING HARDSHIPS

Throughout these various employments, Van Der Zee continued to think about his photography. He had enjoyed success at the

Opposite: James Van Der Zee, *Newstand, Lenox Avenue*, 1925. This photograph captured the hustle and bustle of one of Harlem's main thoroughfares.

Whittier School and entertained the idea of opening a studio. Kate, however, was skeptical and unsupportive. She would say, "No, you'd better get a job. You'll at least know where your money's coming from." To her credit, she had lived on her own since before the two had met and had experienced financial hardship firsthand. Still, Van Der Zee was disheartened. This disagreement was just one of many that would contribute to the couple's unhappiness.

Both had hoped the arrival of their son, Emil, would bring them closer together. Sadly, not even a year after his birth, Emil's life was cut tragically short. Though the Van Der Zees lived in a former luxury apartment, their landlord had grown lax in his duties once the black tenants moved in. The winter of 1908 had been particularly cold, and Emil caught pneumonia and died. As biographer Jim Haskins notes, "His death caused a noticeable crack in a marriage whose foundation had not been very solid to begin with."

In addition to frequent disagreements, Kate wanted to leave every summer to either Buckroe Beach in Hampton, Virginia, or to Portland, Maine. When she left, she would take Rachel and insist that Van Der Zee relinquish their apartment and rent a room somewhere until she returned. During these summers, Van Der Zee would miss Rachel dearly. He had taught her to sing and paint and, as exhibited later through the lens of his camera, he felt a great deal of love for his daughter. Some of Van Der Zee's most touching works are the images of his daughter as a toddler.

Periodically, the three would return to Lenox to visit relatives. During these visits, Van Der Zee would produce exquisite photos of his family, wife, and daughter. Even though he was still an amateur with the camera, the images he created were imbued with a deep compassion for his subjects. Haskins describes these works:

> It is evident that [Van Der Zee] took great care in composing the photographs—selecting the backgrounds, positioning the subjects, taking advantage of the natural play of light

and shade in the outdoor settings. It is also evident that he was very proud of his family, for each person is depicted in a flattering manner ... The finished products are beautifully successful solutions to the problem of compositions, depth, and detail in outdoor light. The ideas are simple, but the close attention to every element in the composition places them far above ordinary photographs.

When most of the Van Der Zee men left for New York, the woman stayed in Lenox. Jennie studied at the Kellogg Art School in Pittsfield, and by 1908, she had married Ernest Toussaint Welcome. Ernest was a businessman who in his lifetime would manage a range of operations including a shoe store, a sight-seeing bus service, a domestic help agency, a realty company, and a magazine called the *Colored American Review*. However, he was most well known for his joint venture with his wife Jennie, the Toussaint Conservatory of Music and Art. This long-time dream of Jennie's became a reality in 1910 when the couple moved to Harlem, at 221 West 134th Street, and set up shop. While the location of the school would change over the years, Jennie's commitment to her students never wavered. The school continued to educate learners until her death in 1956.

The first incarnation of the school operated out of a multi-level Harlem brownstone. The school occupied the first floor and the family lived in the floors above. Van Der Zee created a small studio on the second floor, still pursuing photography as a hobby only.

FAMILY REUNION

With all the additional space, the Welcomes decided to invite their Van Der Zee relatives to live with them. The offer was taken up wholeheartedly; Susan Van Der Zee sold the house in Lenox and brought Charles and Mary with her, while John, Walter, and

James left their apartments to make the move. For the first time in eight years, the Van Der Zees were reunited under one roof.

The happiness, however, was short lived. In one year, the Van Der Zees lost John to tuberculosis, Mary to complications from a fall, and Charles to an unknown affliction. James's two younger siblings' deaths were especially tragic, as Mary was still a teenager and Charles had just reached his twenties. Shortly thereafter, Walter and his family moved out to Jamaica, Queens, where he worked for the Loft Candy Company in Long Island City until his death in 1931.

NEW OPPORTUNITIES

Van Der Zee, Kate, and Rachel moved frequently during this time as well, partly due to Kate's insistence on giving up their apartment every summer she spent away. Between the moves and the family's growing needs, Van Der Zee took on more work of the same stock: operating elevators, waiting at hotels, and playing music. He extended his job search to nearby Newark, New Jersey, until one day in 1915 he noticed an ad in the paper. Van Der Zee recounted:

> Some photographer wanted a darkroom man, and I figured I was "dark" enough for the job! … So I went and answered the ad, and he said he didn't know. He wanted a man who could photograph, too, and he didn't know if his customers would stand for my photographing or not. So—I figured he knew about his business more than I did. A month or so later, I saw another ad. Not knowing it was the same place, I went back again. This time he decided to try me out.

At first, Van Der Zee only worked the darkroom. He would watch his employer quickly and carelessly snap shots of incoming patrons. This lack of consideration and compassion for the photograph and its sitter seemed disgraceful to Van Der Zee. He soon realized his boss had nothing to teach him about the craft and he would only learn through experience. Van Der Zee eagerly waited his chance to take photographs up front.

His opportunity came when Van Der Zee's employer was away for the Jewish holidays. Van Der Zee was left in charge of the shop, despite his employer's nervousness that he might drive business away. If a black photographer did alarm any customers, it didn't last long—Van Der Zee's skills and personable nature won over most clients: "I'd take time with them—you know, sit down and talk to them ahead of time, get their natural expressions and so forth." In fact, people came to prefer Van Der Zee and would leave the studio if he wasn't available to take their picture.

It wasn't long before Van Der Zee began to want more out of his experiences. When he started working as much in the studio as in the darkroom, he asked for a raise. The owner, however, refused. It was then that Van Der Zee thought of opening his own studio. Jennie and Ernest, who were successfully running the Toussaint Conservatory, suggested that he come and work for them by opening a studio in conjunction with the school. Van Der Zee jumped at the idea and opened his first professional studio at the conservatory's new location at 63 West 140th Street.

Immediately he began photographing Harlemites of note. One such sitter was Blanche Powell, the older sister of Adam Clayton Powell Jr., who would later become an influential minister and the first black Congressman from New York. Van Der Zee even had a photo published in the *New York Times*. This image, taken in his youth, was of John E. Parsons, a respected lawyer, establisher of the New York Sugar Trust, and a summer resident of Lenox. However, the photo did little to push his career forward. Van Der Zee continued to operate the photo business part-time, and still worked as a musician and elevator operator to supplement his income. In 1916, he started working for the Chatsworth Apartments, where he would meet his second wife. Gaynella

Greenlee would prove a benefit to Van Der Zee's business, especially in handling management.

A FAMILY SHIFT

His first marriage had been in decline for years, but it grew worse as Van Der Zee began to pursue photography. Kate criticized him for investing in what seemed like a "frivolous and financially unrewarding" side project. They disagreed about most things, and Van Der Zee was growing tired of her habit of leaving every summer: "She'd say she would be gone for a week or two, and then she would stay and stay, and I wouldn't know when she would come back ... So one time I thought I'd put the scare into her. I said, 'Next time you go, don't come back.' And she took me up on it."

Kate returned once more to receive workmen into the apartment so they could move her belongings. Van Der Zee's schedule consisted of working alternating days and nights, so when he returned to the apartment he found it devoid of any trace of Kate. His wife had taken eight-year-old Rachel as well, leaving only a few childhood paintings that Van Der Zee would cherish for the rest of his life. Eventually, Kate and Van Der Zee would get a divorce and he would see Rachel only rarely.

Van Der Zee was depressed for a time, but a developing friendship with a switchboard operator at the Chatsworth Apartments soon lifted his spirits. Gaynella Katz Greenlee, five years his junior, was a beautiful and graceful woman. Their friendship started out innocently enough; Gaynella was a married woman, her husband a "frail, sickly fellow" named Charles Greenlee. Van Der Zee recalls their affection started over food: "She liked to eat and I liked to eat. Lots of maids in the building would give me more food than I could eat, so I'd carry it down to the telephone operator."

Gaynella reciprocated the kind gesture through food as well: "She'd have these nice meals for me ... the food used to taste so good. She was the first person I've seen to cook five or six eggs at a time. I was just used to two eggs, and I said, 'Look! She's got me eating five or six eggs at time!' That was one of the most impressive things she ever did."

Then, in late 1915 or early 1916, Van Der Zee lost his job at the Chatsworth Apartments. This was devastating, as Van Der Zee had unknowingly fallen in love with Gaynella: "She was under the sign of Taurus, and that seems to me a very powerful sign. She was very persuasive, very persevering, and very beautiful. I thought it was quite unusual for such an attractive girl to be so versatile."

Van Der Zee had also become dissatisfied with his business arrangement with Ernest at the Conservatory. So when he suggested the idea of opening his own studio to Gaynella, he was thrilled to find she fully supported it. They decided she would work for him as his secretary, keeping their relationship respectful while Gaynella's husband was still alive and while Van Der Zee's divorce was pending. The two opened the Guarantee Photo Studio in 1915, boasting it could "guarantee customer satisfaction." This would prove to be true for over sixty years. The pair had become not only business partners, but partners for life. In 1916, Gaynella's husband passed away, and shortly thereafter, they were married.

THE KEENEST EYE IN HARLEM

At a time when at-home cameras were rare, the photographer's role was quintessential. Author Deborah Willis writes, "Photography did not discriminate, and its low cost made the portrait available to many." As the custodian for visual memory, the photographer became an integral part to documenting life's most important events. This was even more essential in the black community, for most of its history had only passed down information through oral traditions. With the advent of affordable photography, communities and individuals now had a new means to visually acknowledge and remember their own histories.

James Van Der Zee, *Wedding Party #1*, 1932. Van Der Zee photographed countless families as they celebrated their most important moments, such as weddings.

Van Der Zee quickly became a success in the photo business. He recalls having as many white customers as black, servicing both local Harlem residents and customers from outside the neighborhood. Either through word of mouth or from catching a glimpse of his stunning photographs, sitters flocked to have their picture taken by Van Der Zee. And Van Der Zee, situated in the heart of Harlem during a time of great change, activity, and diversity, captured everything with his lens.

Every major life event needed documenting, including holidays, weddings, and even funerals. Van Der Zee recalls his most lucrative days of the week and times of the year: "The biggest day for studio photos was Sunday ... The high class, the middle class, the poorer class all looked good on Sundays ... Christmastime and Eastertime, graduation time, confirmation time—they were very busy seasons of the year. I was almost too busy to come out of the studio."

He was a renowned wedding photographer; framing couples in his studio to best capture their feelings of joy and hope for the future. He also made compelling family portraits, emphasizing bonds of affection and respect. And he captured funerary images of the deceased, often incorporating religious imagery and poetry to lessen the pain of death. He was known for his exquisite retouching techniques and use of haunting photographic overlays (techniques to be discussed in Chapter 4). However, most of all, Van Der Zee became known about town as "the picture-takin' man," the photographer with the keenest eye in all of Harlem.

Part of what made Van Der Zee's images so compelling was the natural, emotive qualities he brought out in his sitters. With each picture he tried to create a story. Van Der Zee described it as making them "appear to be doing something, not just sitting there posing for the picture." Children playing the piano beside proud, onlooking parents, dancers mid-pose, families gathered in a living room conversing: these were just some of the scenes Van Der Zee would create for his sitters. His "active insertion of a narrative interpretation into the photo" helped elevate his images from simple snapshots to works of art.

THROUGH THE PHOTOGRAPHER'S LENS

James Van Der Zee's most lucrative work was in portraiture. Entertainers of all kinds came through his door: band leaders, actresses, models, musicians, comedians, and Harlem celebrities. Singer Florence Mills, Harlem's first international superstar, posed for him. When she died, he photographed her funeral as well. He photographed Jack Johnson, the first black world heavyweight boxing champion. He took a portrait of Madame Walker, the first female business owner to become a millionaire in the United States, and her daughter A'Lelia, businesswoman and patron of the arts. The names on his list of clients are astounding: Joe Louis, the famous boxer; Hazel Scott, the pianist and singer; Bill "Bojangles" Robinson, the dancer and film star; Satchel Paige, the baseball player; Countee

Cullen, the poet; and countless others. All of these people came to James Van Der Zee to create stunning portfolio pieces.

But it wasn't just celebrities who enjoyed the benefit of Van Der Zee's lens. Whether Boy Scouts, beauticians, or bouncing babies, all walks of life in Harlem received the star treatment from Mr. Van Der Zee's photographic eye:

> It seemed I had a personal interest in the pictures I made, and I did my best to make them as good as I could. And if they were satisfactory to me, then I just kept them. Sometimes they seemed to be more valuable to me than they did to the people I was photographing, because I put my heart and soul into them and tried to see that every picture was better looking than the person.

Each subject was deserving of Van Der Zee's attention. Each finished print showed the artist's compassion for making beautiful images from his uniquely beautiful subjects.

James Van Der Zee's photographic work was not just relegated to the studio. He often shot subjects in their homes, shining a light onto how the black middle class of Harlem really lived. These images depict families living in comfort, proud and optimistic, embodying the American dream, or the concept that prosperity and social mobility is available to all Americans. He also photographed the streets, documenting the many religious, social, and civic organizations that were an integral part of Harlem life. The list of civic and fraternal organizations is just as extensive as his portraiture and includes the Elks, Masons (of which he was a member), black fraternities like Alpha Phi Alpha, and black athletic teams. He photographed schools, churches, and religious figures. His images of Father Divine, Daddy Grace, Reverend Adam Clayton Powell Sr. and Jr., Rabbi Matthews of the Zionist Temple in Harlem, and others captured a climate of religious diversity and participation that was central to black culture.

James Van Der Zee, *Dancer*, 1925. Harlem's most glamorous and talented had portraits taken at the G.G.G. Studio.

James Van Der Zee shot this portrait of a member of Marcus Garvey's African Legion (*left, in uniform*) and his family, titled *Garveyite Family*, 1924.

Van Der Zee also shot images for photo calendars. The Eastman Kodak Company referred clients to him who requested quality photographs of black subjects. This quickly became a very lucrative market for Van Der Zee. Sometimes he arrived at these images through everyday clients; if a portrait turned out well, he would ask the sitter to sign a waiver. Other times, he staged models in his studio specifically for the purpose of calendar shots. These photos are often recognizable by their lofty narratives, theatrical costumes, and strong sense of sentiment. He liked to create "little home scenes," which depicted heartwarming domestic settings. Occasionally he would photograph nudes, highlighting the model's natural beauty through sensitive use of light and shadow.

WORKING THE WORLD WARS

Van Der Zee also saw a boost in work during the two World Wars. Van Der Zee himself had never been drafted, though at one point Kate tried, out of anger, to write the draft board on his behalf. Van Der Zee never had any intentions of enlisting: "*No thank you! Nobody* had done anything to me at *no* time. To go over there and look for a fight—that was not for me. This mother's child was not ready to be a soldier!"

What Van Der Zee did, in addition to working in an ammunition plant for a short while, was take photographs of soldiers and their families: "The boys used to have their pictures made before they went over, and then their mothers and fathers and girlfriends would have their pictures made and sent to their boys." His photographs capture the complexity of a soldier's state of mind. In their faces we can see courage and pride, but also an anxiety toward leaving their loved ones behind.

Needham Roberts was one of these soldiers. A member of the Harlem Hellfighters, Roberts was one of the first Americans to be awarded the French Croix de Guerre in war in 1918. Passed up for the Purple Heart in his lifetime because of his race, he was posthumously decorated in 1996.

James Van Der Zee, *Daddy Grace and Children*, 1938. An influential figure in Harlem, Daddy Grace's portrait embodies the preacher's flare for the dramatic. Van Der Zee incorporated additional religious iconography through photomontage.

As the official photographer of the UNIA, Van Der Zee took this picture of Marcus Garvey (*center, wearing the fringed hat*), titled *Marcus Garvey in Regalia*, 1924.

In 1924, Van Der Zee was asked to be the official photographer for Marcus Garvey's **Universal Negro Improvement Association (UNIA)**. These photographs serve as an important historical marker, capturing the spirit and hope of **Black Nationalism** in the 1920s. Members of UNIA marched in parades, performed drills as apart of auxiliary and guard corps for the African Legion, and attended conventions to discuss the state of African diaspora. Van Der Zee captured these grand moments, as well as regal images of Marcus Garvey himself.

CHANGING WITH THE TIMES

The 1920s were a time of great social and cultural change, but also technological changes. By that time, Van Der Zee had transitioned

THE PICTURE-TAKIN' MAN

Jim Haskins, Van Der Zee's most intimate biographer, titled his book *The Picture Takin' Man*. All of Harlem knew him by this name. But where did the nickname come from?

It was a usual day at the studio with Gaynella managing the front desk and Van Der Zee working in the back. While on a break, Van Der Zee glanced at the barbershop across the street and told Gaynella he was going out for a cut and shave. "If anyone should come in to be photographed," he said, "send a boy over to let me know." Often, Gaynella would take photographs for Van Der Zee while he stepped out. However, if she was busy and he was close by, she would enlist one of the neighborhood boys to fetch him. No sooner had the barber put the towel around Van Der Zee's neck did a young man come busting through the door.

Van Der Zee remembers: "In comes the kid—I think they called him Hercules. He started running up and down the aisle, calling, 'The picture-takin' man here? The picture-takin' man here?'"

The barber pointed to Van Der Zee and the kid rushed to him. Hercules placed one hand on the chair, crossed his legs, and said, "Are you the picture-takin' man? Well, uh, uh, the picture-takin' lady said, 'Tell the picture-takin' man to come over to the picture-takin' place. Somebody wants their picture taken.'" From then on, the name stuck!

from using glass plates to film: "Plates are no good. You drop one of them and your whole career is gone, practically. And then, of course, they're very heavy. You get eight or ten of those things, you got all you can carry."

From here on out, Van Der Zee used larger-format film for portraits and smaller film for location shots. Honing his skills from years of experience, he was now able to use a range of cameras and lenses to his advantage. His craftsmanship had finally caught up with his vision but, like a true artist, he would continue to push himself: "When it came to photography, I can't recall ever trying to do anything I [couldn't] do, but at the same time I was never satisfied. I was always trying to do better."

However, during the height of Van Der Zee's popularity, tragedy struck. In 1927, his daughter, Rachel, aged nineteen, died of appendicitis while in Portland, Maine. As a last gesture of love, Van Der Zee photographed her funeral, incorporating poems and heavenly imagery into the final prints. It was after her death that Van Der Zee finally lost track of his ex-wife Kate. Rachel had been the remaining tie between them, and with her gone, Van Der Zee closed that chapter of his life. He had a new life, one that would center on his wife Gaynella and photography for more than fifty years.

MAKING A BUSINESS

The year Rachel died was also the year that Van Der Zee and Gaynella decided to incorporate the photography business. They hired a lawyer to help sort out the paperwork but were immediately told they needed to change the name: "He said the only ones who could use the name Guarantee were banks and trust companies, so we had to pick a new one. I decided to name it after my wife. Her name was Gaynella, and when I met her it was Gaynella Greenlee—G.G.—so I added another G. and called it the G.G.G. Photo Studio."

James Van Der Zee, Self-portrait, circa 1918.

This decision came easy, as Van Der Zee was not interested in promoting his name. He preferred to live a secluded life and felt branding himself would be vain: "People didn't even know who James Van Der Zee was, only knew that I was the 'picture-takin' man.' Most everyone called me that. The cops used to call me Michelangelo."

Van Der Zee did, however, sign many of his photographs. He figured using a signature was just good business: it marked his handiwork and directed potential clients to his studio. Typically, Van Der Zee would shoot three poses during a sitting. The client usually selected one of the photographs to be signed. However, sometimes a photograph would go unsigned, at the request of the client. Van Der Zee's signature move was often the many different ways he signed his last name, on photographs and on official documents. Sometimes it was VanDerZee. Other times Vanderzee, and others Van Der Zee. This later resulted in many different historians, journalists, and biographers also spelling his last name in a variety of ways.

Luckily for historians, Van Der Zee retained a copy of all his negatives and prints. He felt if a photograph was up to his artistic standards, it was worthy of being kept. These hundreds of plates, negatives, and prints would prove an invaluable and rare record of Harlem many years later.

Despite being the man who chronicled some of the most important people, moments, and movements of the Harlem Renaissance, Van Der Zee came away with no stories to tell: "I had an assignment to make the job, I'd make the job, and I'd be gone. That was it."

Van Der Zee was apolitical and unmoved by celebrities. While this may be "maddening for historians," it seems the perfect disposition for a documentarian. Van Der Zee had been the "picture-takin' man" of Harlem, no more, and no less.

CHAPTER THREE

THE LATER YEARS

The booming success of the 1920s soon ended and by the mid-1930s business was significantly slower. Gaynella had picked out their first studio location, a former auto garage with ample room and great foot traffic from the street. However, after the Great Depression hit, the studio proved unaffordable. They moved to two smaller locations before settling on a studio/apartment at 272 Lenox Avenue. They would call this building home from 1943 to 1968.

There had been a burst of business at the onset of World War II, but overall, photography jobs had become scarcer. By 1945, most people owned their own cameras, relegating studio photography to special events or official, utilitarian uses. Van Der Zee continued shooting his usual portrait, school and church, and calendar images but took on less creatively fulfilling work to pay the bills. He shot passport photos and documented scenes for insurance purposes, snapping grisly images of autopsies and auto damage. He worked for a mail-order business, retouching

Opposite: James Van Der Zee, *Beautician in the Beauty Parlor*, 1924.

and restoring old photographs that were sent in. To make extra cash, the Van Der Zees also rented out their extra rooms to boarders. These measures quelled financial pressures for a while. However, money always seemed to disappear faster than it came. Gaynella had a weakness for shopping, and Van Der Zee was notorious for lending cash to friends in need, most of whom would never pay him back.

LOSS

The 1930s also began a series of family losses for Van Der Zee. His mother, Susan, died one week before her seventy-fifth birthday in 1931. Shortly thereafter, Van Der Zee's brother Walter passed on and was quickly followed by Ernest Welcome, Van Der Zee's brother-in-law. Van Der Zee's sister, Jennie, continued to run her late husband's businesses and the Toussaint Conservatory of Art and Music until her own death in 1956. When Jennie passed away, Van Der Zee was distraught: "She went to the hospital expecting to come out, to go back home. They said she was full of cancer … [and] I had an autopsy done because I couldn't understand and [didn't] believe it … I had to close up the [conservatory] and I kept thinking about that yard so full of children."

It wasn't just Van Der Zee's family experiencing hard times: Harlem was becoming a slum. The black population had steadily increased, and by World War II, the neighborhood was grossly overcrowded. The once large, new, and luxurious apartments that had made Harlem a beacon of hope for middle-class families were now subdivided by landlords into smaller, poorly maintained spaces. The city did little in the 1950s or 1960s to address problems that had turned neighborhoods into ghettos: potholes and trash littered the streets, schools were not given adequate supplies, and racial and class tensions were on the rise. Hostilities came to a head during the **Harlem Riot of 1964**. The riots, which had started in reaction to a police shooting of two black youths,

Protestors during the March on Washington for Jobs and Freedom,
Washington, DC, 1963.

expanded to include almost four thousand rioters and set off a chain of riots in other American cities such as Philadelphia, Rochester, and Chicago. Almost overnight Harlem had become a war zone. Van Der Zee and Gaynella witnessed it firsthand from their storefront studio:

> You could hear window glasses crash every now and then. We managed to save the store next to us, the grocery store. But there were other stores that lost everything to the looters. There were people passing by with all kinds of things ... A guy came by a few days later wearing a suit of clothes that didn't fit him very well. He said it was his "riot suit"—got it at the time of the riot. They had all kinds of jokes like that, but I couldn't very well see their point of view ... I wouldn't have any part of it.

The tragic events of the riots happened concurrent to the passing of the **Civil Rights Act of 1964**. This legislation outlawed any type of discrimination based on race, color, religion, sex, or national origin and required that all public spaces be free of racial segregation. This bill was a landmark achievement for civil equality and would serve the American people in innumerable positive ways.

However, for the Van Der Zee household, this bill meant a loss of quality boarders. Many of their "high-class roomers" left for safer neighborhoods and fancier apartment complexes, places that had once been available only to white renters. They began to see a shift in renters from middle-class workers to tenants who were unemployed, on welfare, and uninterested in improving the condition of the house. Once, for no reason, a mentally unstable tenant began burning newspapers on the floor. Luckily he was stopped before extensive damage was done, but the message was clear: even their own home wasn't safe from the chaos on the streets. Van Der Zee and Gaynella were growing older and vulnerable, unable to defend against those who might do them harm: "It ... was pretty hard to do business [when] you had to keep the door locked until you could see who wanted to come in ... One time [thieves] broke into the back, another time through the skylight in the roof ... the last time they just threw a rock through the front door and came on in."

Luckily neither Gaynella nor Van Der Zee was hurt during these break-ins. But the Harlem they had known and loved had transformed into a frightening place. They had become unknowing prisoners in their own home: they did not want to go, but even if they had, their financial situation and aging health would have stopped them.

In 1967, the Van Der Zees attempted to buy their studio and apartment. Gaynella felt she would be unable to secure a mortgage from a bank so instead she turned to a loan shark. The fees were so high that the couple pawned off many of their possessions just to keep up with payments. Within eleven months, the financial strain had become unbearable. To make matters worse, Gaynella realized that her payments did not include taxes or additional fees. She was unable to cope and abruptly stopped making payments.

The apartment began to go into foreclosure. Van Der Zee scrambled to get a second mortgage but ran into more dirty dealing:

> I went to my bank ... and they gave me commitment papers for a second mortgage. I gave them to an ex-judge named Mr. Stout, who I thought was a friend of mine, to arrange the closing, and he wound up with the title of the place in his name ... [then] he started sending people by the house to look at the place. Every time we refused to let somebody look through the place he'd serve us with a seventy-two-hour eviction notice, and that upset my wife, kind of brought on a nervous breakdown.

Harlem daytime activity, circa 1940.

Shortly thereafter, Van Der Zee discovered his own lawyer had purchased the Van Der Zee brownstone. Unsympathetic, the lawyer soon had the police forcibly evict the Van Der Zees. The scene was horrendous: Gaynella screamed so violently that she was tied to a chair and then sent to the Harlem Hospital. Meanwhile, the marshal and his deputies searched the home, forcing Van Der Zee to illegally sign over to them $1,800 worth of traveler's checks and un-cashed social security checks. In the end, they left Van Der Zee with $20 and Gaynella with mental trauma that would stay with her for the remainder of her life.

Their belongings were placed in storage and community workers began showing them housing options. Because they had failed to pay their mortgage, they did not qualify for city assistance, so it was up to Van Der Zee to find an affordable apartment. He chose a small one-bedroom apartment on the Upper West Side of Manhattan and tried his best to make the new space feel like home. However, Gaynella was unresponsive:

> I really thought she would recuperate, but she was never straight after we were evicted … She didn't take an interest in anything … She used to follow those morning TV programs, and for quite a while she followed the funnies in the paper; but she [soon] lost all interest … She used to have a good memory. Then all of a sudden she couldn't remember one day from the other, couldn't remember much of anything … She kind of lost her hearing, lost her eyesight … She really didn't want to get well. I could see her fading like a rose.

For eight years Gaynella remained this way. Van Der Zee recalls she was "no trouble to live with … [but] she also wasn't herself." Her condition was especially heartbreaking because it came at a time when Van Der Zee's photographs were being "discovered." His life would split in two directions, his career skyrocketing while his personal life declined. The contrast was stark; the Van Der Zees were evicted from their home the same year Van Der Zee's work first appeared in the Metropolitan Museum of Art. Despite these hardships, he was able to recognize that "things which seem to be a curse sometimes are a blessing in disguise." Van Der Zee soon found that these dark times gave way to a personal and creative renaissance.

FINDING SUCCESS

In 1967, a researcher from the Metropolitan Museum of Art contacted Van Der Zee. Reginald McGhee had been charged with finding photographs that stood in contrast to popular perception that Harlem was, and had always been, a downtrodden place.

These images would be a part of an exhibition that aimed to highlight the beauty, pride, and contributions of Harlem residents to American culture at large. This led McGhee to the humble, small studio of the elderly James Van Der Zee.

Exhibition catalogue for controversial *Harlem On My Mind*.

James Van Der Zee

HARLEM ON MY MIND

The exhibition that catapulted Van Der Zee into the public eye was one of the most infamous shows of the twentieth century. The drama, however, had nothing to do with Van Der Zee's photos. The Met's director Thomas Hoving hired curator Allan Schoener to create an exhibition that would challenge viewers. Using a model that proved successful at the Jewish Museum, Schoener created a "multimedia extravaganza that was virtually unheard of at the time." He incorporated blown-up photographs, music and sound recordings, and extensive wall text. Today, this type of exhibition design is commonly used in history or science museums because it creates an immersive experience. However, since this was the museum's first exhibition celebrating the work of black artists, the result felt more like "anthropology, not art." No paintings or sculptures created by Harlem Renaissance artists were included. Most shocking of all was that the exhibition catalogue essay contained **anti-Semitic** and racist comments. Written as a term paper by a high school student, the essay incorporated research from a sociological study on race relations. However, when taken out of context, it sounded like hate propaganda. Protests began even before the exhibition opened and, in the first nine days, more than seventy-five thousand visitors came to see the controversy. In the end, Van Der Zee's work, compelling and without pretense, shone through the drama.

As the researcher began to sort through the hundreds of incredible photographs Van Der Zee had saved over the years, he could "hardly contain is excitement." Van Der Zee, however, was not as thrilled. He cooperated but didn't expect this exchange to propel his career forward. Magazines, galleries, and individuals had asked to look at his materials in the past. His work had even been published in the *New York Times* and *Esquire* magazine, but nothing ever came of these opportunities. When he first gave the researchers access to his negatives and prints, he didn't give it much thought and assumed it was just "another advertising stunt."

However, much to his surprise, the exhibit *Harlem On My Mind* opened at the Met in 1969 and was an astounding success. While the exhibition was made up of different artists' work, Van Der Zee was the single largest contributor. The photos spanned his artistic career and presented a vision of Harlem that most of the world had forgotten and many more were unaware of. Featured were his images of infamous figures such as Marcus Garvey and Daddy Grace, group portraits of social and fraternal organizations, and depictions of middle-class, aspiring Harlemites. Visitors were stunned that the majority of these images came from one photographer's lens. Almost overnight, James Van Der Zee, newly "discovered" at age eighty-three, had become a legend of the craft.

Visitors and researchers flocked to Van Der Zee to learn more about the mysterious photographer. As biographer Haskins describes it, "All of a sudden the modest man who had lived his life in relative obscurity was so feted and honored that he hardly knew what to make of it." Furthermore, he began earning money from his photographs in a way he never knew possible:

The Met paid me ... just for the pictures they had used, that I'd already been paid for by the clients, and that didn't earn that much for me probably in the whole year I was making them! Then they began publishing these books. Two thousand dollars advance royalties from Grove Press. And seven hundred and seventy-five dollars for the pictures used in the *Harlem On My Mind* book. So, the picture business began to get very interesting!

Both the exhibition catalogue for *Harlem On My Mind* and *The World of James Van Der Zee: A Visual Record of Black America* by Grove Press were published in 1969. He was soon honored by the American Society of Magazine Photographers, was elected as a member of the National Geographic Society, and received an award of merit from the Photographers Forum. These books and accolades helped to further publicize the importance of the photographer's work.

THE INSTITUTE

Offers began pouring in to buy the entirety of the Van Der Zee portfolio. Bids came in at upwards of $175,000, but Van Der Zee, unsure of how to respond, turned to Reginald McGhee for guidance. He told Van Der Zee to turn down these initial offers, and in 1969, he and Charles Inniss, director of the Studio Museum in Harlem, founded the James Van Der Zee Institute. Van Der Zee signed over approximately 54,139 works to the institute, unaware that their value was an estimated $10 million. Van Der Zee would later describe this decision as a mistake: "There was so much confusion at that time. I did whatever I was asked to do. I did not have a lawyer or anyone else to represent me."

The institute was formed to care for the Van Der Zee collection as well as to highlight the work of young black photographers. They organized Van Der Zee's first solo exhibition at the public library in his hometown of Lenox, Massachusetts. Between 1970 and 1972, they organized an additional eleven exhibitions of his work. They even published a newsletter that showcased both Van Der Zee's collection and emerging photographers' portfolios.

However, the institute had a hard time affording its overhead and had to eventually sell off parts of its collection. The biggest buyer was the Metropolitan Museum of Art, which purchased seventy photographs.

The Met would soon be formative to the institute in other ways. For many years, the institute was housed and funded by the Met, until circumstances in 1978 caused the institute to move. The institute and the remainder of the Van Der Zee collection were eventually absorbed into the Studio Museum in Harlem.

While the Van Der Zee Institute initially helped Van Der Zee bring his work to the public, it soon became clear that it would be the sole beneficiary of any sales or publications of his work going forward. In 1980, however, a long legal battle started for the rights to his photographs. Van Der Zee himself filed a formal suit against the Studio Museum, but it was not settled until after his death in 1984. Van Der Zee felt while he gained public recognition and compensation, he received little else:

> The institute did not protect my work and did not provide me with financial support as I had expected. For example, McGhee told me that he had to sell some of the work to pay the institute's rent. As to financial assistance, I received a carfare, a suit and a turkey from McGhee. These were certainly not enough to live on … I did not intend to permanently transfer my collections. My intentions [were] completely frustrated.

THE REBIRTH OF THE ARTIST

However, unlike when he lost his home, this time Van Der Zee had allies to help him. In 1975, Harlem resident Ruth Sherman organized the Friends of James Van Der Zee, with the mission of helping the artist pay his bills and look into Van Der Zee's eviction. The club, mainly women, threw fundraising parties and managed his storage and rent invoices. True to their namesake, these women were friends to Van Der Zee. He once said, "You'd be surprised how many cards I get from them!" The Friends of James Van Der Zee would provide logistical, financial, emotional, and even creative support for him in his remaining years.

In 1976, a member of the Friends of James Van Der Zee, Camille Billops, collaborated with Van Der Zee on two projects. A visual artist, filmmaker, and historian in her own right, Camille organized a fundraiser event for Van Der Zee's first formal portrait session since 1969. There, he photographed contemporary artists and icons of culture. This even featured a sitting of painter Benny Andrews. Later that year, Van Der Zee, Billops, and Owen Dodson also began work on a book, later to be published as *The Harlem Book of the Dead*.

However, also that year, after eight years of mental decline and just a few days before Van Der Zee's ninetieth birthday, Gaynella passed away. Van Der Zee was devastated. "I loved that woman. When she was young, she was beautiful, and she became beautiful for me afterwards because I loved her. Through all the thick and thin years and the in-between years, deeper than the deepest oceans, a love taller than the tallest tree, that's the way it was for me. And I think she left me with a song that will never end."

This was the first time he was too upset to use his camera; he asked for a photographer named Frank Stewart to photograph her funeral for him. The image was nice, but in true form, Van Der Zee hoped he could make some "improvements" by integrating angelic images and verses into the picture. It is unclear if he ever made these changes, but he did frame the photo and kept it surrounded by flowers in remembrance.

During Gaynella's years of mental anguish, she had missed the triumphs and accolades Van Der Zee was receiving for his lifetime of work. His sudden rise to fame had terrible timing. Van Der Zee felt "it was too much, too late," noting that if he only had been contacted a few years earlier, perhaps he could

Jean-Michel Basquiat, 1982.

have prevented losing his home and his wife. Van Der Zee was tired; he was ninety years old living a life he didn't recognize anymore. He fell into a depression and stopped caring for his own health and home. Even the Friends of James Van Der Zee could not pull him from his sadness. However, Van Der Zee still had more heights to reach and more artwork to make before his time would come. Even more miraculously, he had one more great love to experience.

Donna Mussenden met Van Der Zee in August 1975. She was thirty years old, had worked for a time as a caseworker, and was serving as the director of the National Urban League's Art Gallery. When first introduced to Van Der Zee, she found he was living in "a drab and unkempt flat, lame, broke, and in bad health." In fact, he barely had his eyesight. Cataracts had clouded most of the sight from both of his eyes. Donna was appalled by his condition: "I asked myself, is this how we treat our cultural giants? Is this what we give to geniuses who have given everything they have to us?"

So she set to work. She first helped him clean up his apartment, organizing his files and making his home livable again. Then she helped Van Der Zee improve his health, regulating his diet, cooking his meals, and eventually encouraging him to have cataract surgery at the age of ninety-two. Finally, she helped him feel hopeful for the future. In 1978, the two were wed in his one-bedroom apartment with a small number of family and friends attending. However, they kept their marriage secret at first. "We attended many, many events I had orchestrated as his assistant where no one knew we were married," said Donna.

Van Der Zee found new energy, invigorating his career. In 1978, *The Harlem Book of the Dead* was published. In 1980, Van Der Zee produced a new series of portraits, this time with even more illustrious subjects. Some of his sitters included Jean-Michel Basquiat (who in return painted a portrait of Van Der Zee), Muhammad Ali, Romare Bearden, Cicely Tyson, Miles Davis, Ossie Davis, Ruby Dee, and Bill Cosby. They all sat in the penthouse apartment he and Donna by that time had moved into. Van Der Zee's original camera, equipment, props, and furniture were used in these portraits. A theatrical set designer painted backdrops similar to those used in Van Der Zee's original photographs, right on his apartment terrace.

Van Der Zee continued to actively photograph until his death. He often joked that, due to his age, he had to create work on "the installment plan," working at a pace that made sense. But that didn't mean he wasn't engaged, as he explained: "The body wears out, but the mind don't need to."

THE FINAL YEARS

Van Der Zee had now become a legend in his field. He and Donna traveled the United States, making public appearances, attending exhibitions, and accepting awards. Van Der Zee, who left school at age fourteen, received four honorary doctorates from Seton Hall University, Haverford College, Columbia College Chicago,

Irving Penn, *James Van Der Zee, New York, February 11, 1983*

and Donna's alma mater, Howard University. He was the subject of a documentary entitled *Uncommon Images: The Harlem of James VanDerZee*, in which he spoke freely about his experiences in photography and life. He participated in countless exhibitions, and his work was acquired by some of the most prestigious museums in the world. He was the recipient of a Lifetime Fellowship Award from the Metropolitan Museum of Art. President Jimmy Carter presented him with the Living Legacy Award for his contributions to the history of African-American life. Countless more books and biographies featuring Van Der Zee's work and life story were published in the subsequent years. Van Der Zee's legacy would be preserved and celebrated for years to come, even after the death of the artist himself.

The evening he accepted his doctorate from Howard University, James Van Der Zee had a heart attack. He was quickly rushed to the hospital but was unresponsive. On May 15, 1983, at 2:30 a.m., James Van Der Zee was pronounced dead. The artist was ninety-six years old.

The funeral was held on May 20, at Riverside Church in Morningside Heights, New York City. Because in New York City you could not have pallbearers carry the casket, Donna arranged for photographers and others close to her husband to process into the church and sit in an area especially for them. Among the honored speakers that day were Dr. James Cheek, president of Howard University; Reverand Dr. Wyatt T. Walker; and Regina Perry, art historian. His body was entombed in the crypt at Trinity Cemetery and Mausoleums at Broadway and 155th Street.

At the time of his passing, the artist's list of accomplishments was great. More than this, however, James Van Der Zee would be remembered for the compassion and vision he expressed through his camera lens. Since his passing, his wife Donna has continued to promote her late husband's works, his name, and his reputation, ensuring that generations of future photographers do not forget the great man that was James Van Der Zee.

PART II

The Works of James Van Der Zee

"Being an artist, I had an artist's instincts … You can see the picture before it's taken; then it's up to you to get the camera to see."

—*James Van Der Zee*

Opposite: James Van Der Zee, *Couple in Raccoon Coats,* 1932.

CHAPTER FOUR

THE ARTIST'S AND THE CAMERA'S EYE

In his lifetime James Van Der Zee would see the world change dramatically. He witnessed empires rise and fall, civil rights movements take hold, and popular culture transform through movies, television, music, and fashion. But for Van Der Zee, nothing embodied these transformations like the evolution of photography. The artist worked with photographic equipment for over eighty-four years. In his lifetime, the medium, and its meaning in people's lives, would change dramatically.

THE EVOLUTION OF PHOTOGRAPHY

The word "photography" comes from the Greek roots *photos* and *graphé*, meaning "drawing with light." Photography is the process by which light imprints an image onto a chemically treated surface. When Van Der Zee first started taking photos in the year 1900, the standard surface was a **dry plate**, also known as a gelatin plate. In 1879, George Eastman, pioneer and namesake of Eastman Kodak, industrialized the plate coating system, thereby making dry plate

Opposite: James Van Der Zee, *Secretary,* 1929.

photography the most widely available and financially affordable method for its time. The dry plate process captured images onto glass plates, slightly thinner than a windowpane, which had been coated with a dry emulsion chemical. The end result was a finely detailed but extremely delicate negative that could be used in a dark room to make enlarged multiples.

While plate photography continued to be used for astronomical purposes as late as the 1990s, around the 1930s the industry standard switched from plate to film photography. Film was lighter, less cumbersome, and nowhere near as fragile as glass. Additionally, film was more sensitive to light and could record more information. The measurement that is used today to judge a film stock's sensitivity is called the **ISO**, or film speed. A higher film speed meant a greater range of **values**, or lightness and darkness, in an image. Consider the vast improvement of technology: When Van Der Zee started using glass plates, the average ISO was only 40. Within his own lifetime, film speeds increased to 1,000 ISO. Today, with the advent of digital cameras, there are units that unofficially rank as high as 40,000.

It wasn't just film that changed in Van Der Zee's lifetime. Lighting techniques and the use of flash evolved as well. Van Der Zee recalled a time when he had to ignite flash powder to light his images: "If you put too much powder in, why, you were liable to blow your head off, or at least your hand. I knew people who got burned pretty bad."

Different apparatuses were developed to avoid this hazard. Van Der Zee eventually purchased a device that worked by lighting a match, placing it through a partition with a hole in it, and dropping the flame into a tray full of powder. Other methods even involved shooting a gun with a cap into a tray of powder. It wasn't just safety that made the flash powder troublesome: "You'd open the lens of the camera, let the powder go off—bang!—and close the camera up. 'Course there was a great deal of smoke afterwards. If there was a high ceiling it was all right because it took a little time for the powder to go up and come down. I'd try to make a second shot quick, because when all that smoke came down everyone would start coughing and choking."

Eventually, these methods would change: "Some ... had flash bags they put the powder in, and had it connected up with electricity. Flash went off, and it wasn't so bad. Then later on, they came up with the flash bulbs and that was a great improvement. There wasn't any smoke."

And those would give way to others: "After the district began changing from DC to AC current, why, most everything was fluorescent lights, which were very good because they were less expensive, and you didn't have to worry about them blowing out—carbon light blew out very easily."

Most incredibly, Van Der Zee saw the medium transition from an expensive craft to a household hobby. When he first started out, he mixed his own chemical developers because the commercially available solutions were too expensive. Eventually, these developers became affordable. By the end of his lifetime, Van Der Zee would be able to use the first mass market, "point-and-shoot" camera, also known as the Instamatic. He would also see a camera that could develop its own photographs instantly, the Polaroid. His opinion of these was less than stellar: "With the first Polaroids, lots of people had bad judgment. They'd overdevelop and overtime them. But then they began making cameras that people couldn't make mistakes with. Now they have cameras that take the picture and it develops itself. It's remarkable the amount of brains that some people must have."

There is a concrete link between an artist's tools and his or her vision. As technology changed, so did a photographer's approach to image making. It can be argued that the style of photography from the 1800s to the early 1900s was born out of the laborious process inherent with early photographic equipment. James Van Der Zee, while a self-taught artist with no "direct contact with any of the artistic movements of the era," stumbled upon many of the same techniques popular during this time, though he continued to work with them well past the turn of the century.

Perhaps Van Der Zee used these techniques because he faced the same technological challenges, experimenting and manipulating aspects of the photographic process to arrive at comparable ends. Or perhaps, as curator Colin Westerbeck puts it, "He just adapted to his own needs whatever styles of photography he had been exposed to in the genteel world in which his tastes were formed." Whatever the case was, Van Der Zee's portrait style had elements of Victorian, Edwardian, and Pictorial traditions. However, while Van Der Zee's would carry these unconscious influences, his large body of work would stretch beyond this to something uniquely his own.

FINDING HIS STYLE

Pictorialism was the predominant aesthetic at the turn of the century. Truly the first international, photographic art movement, Pictorialism strove to promote photography as art by imbuing it with painterly and hand-manipulated elements. They felt that photography could only be taken seriously as an art form if it followed in other mediums' footsteps; either in subject matter or through the physical manipulation of the negatives or prints.

For outdoor photography, this translated as pastoral or naturalistic scenes, mimicking designs found in classical paintings. For portrait photography, this meant loftier narratives; anything that invoked allegorical themes or classical elegance was incorporated. Photographers employed a soft focus or blurred images in the printing process in order to enhance the dreamlike qualities. Pictoralism was a movement steeped in "exaggerated sentimentality," and created works that ranged from hauntingly beautiful to picturesque and superficial.

This style of photography, especially in portraiture, worked well with early technology because it emphasized the beauty of stillness. Slow film speeds could not capture movement without significant blurring, and so models had to remain motionless. Often in early portraiture you will see sitters with emotionless faces—this would have been the easiest expression to hold throughout the long exposure time. Since these photographs were unable to utilize the visual drama that comes from movement, they relied heavily on compelling backgrounds, props, and even photo manipulation to excite the eye.

Speed and exposure time had already improved when Van Der Zee began using photographic equipment. However, for more aesthetic reasons, Van Der Zee also utilized theatrical elements in his portraiture. In Harlem he collaborated with the little-known artist Edward "Eddie" Elcha. A magnificent painter and photographer in his own right, Elcha created the illusionistic backgrounds for most of Van Der Zee's pictures. However, unlike the Pictorialists, who created beautiful images for beauty's sake, Van Der Zee always had his sitters in mind. His work may have utilized photographic tropes from the nineteenth century, but his aim was inadvertently much more modern. He wanted to bring out the unique beauty of each of his subjects: "I posed everybody according to their type and personality, and therefore almost every picture was different … In the majority of studios, they just seem to pose everybody the same according to custom, according to fashion, and therefore the pictures seem to be mechanical-looking to me."

It is the naturalism and honesty he drew out of his subjects that set his work apart from his peers. Photographer Dawoud Bey elaborates on James Van Der Zee's ability to pose his sitters:

James Van Der Zee was a master at coaxing an infinite variety of physically expressive gestures from his subjects. The portrait photographer confronting the human subject quickly comes to realize that a bit of coaching is necessary if one doesn't simply want to make the same picture over and over again. Van Der Zee's ability to continually reinvent the vocabulary of human gesture, while retaining the strong sense of personhood in each of his subjects, provides evidence of a rich and creative imagination.

He photographed people from all walks of life, from different backgrounds, professions, and ages, but he was always able to show them in their best light. His approach was both conceptual and literal: "Before taking them, I would figure out the best angle to try and get as much light and expression and character in the picture as possible."

Van Der Zee further differentiated himself from the earlier styles through his work created outside of the studio. Unlike Pictorial photographers, whose "reliance on a modest repertoire of subject matter and image treatment produced a homogeneous aesthetic," Van Der Zee's photos captured life in Harlem through a diversity of means.

His photos of public parades, storefronts, and social events are more akin to street photography in the way they capture a single moment. Photographer Dorothea Lange described this phenomenon in photography as taking "an instant out of time, altering life by holding it still." Different still was Van Der Zee's approach to shooting images of fraternal organizations, sports teams, and church groups. These pictures are documentarian like; they present the subjects in a matter-of-fact way.

His most compelling "non-studio" photos are the revealing portraits of sitters in their own homes. These photographs are deeply intimate, allowing the viewer a glimpse into each subject's private life. One image, *A Man in His Bedroom*, depicts a man sitting off to one side, "invisible because his ornate dressing gown blends in with the wealth of patterned surfaces in the room." The second photo from Van Der Zee's *Heiress* series reveals a woman almost engulfed by her elegant and luxurious surroundings. At first glance she appears out of place, but a closer look reveals a

James Van Der Zee, *The Heiress #2,* 1938. This photograph is one of many by Van Der Zee that depict an optimistic and socially mobile black middle class.

confident, unshakable expression. She is the new owner of this home, inheriting it from her employers who she worked for for many years.

MASTERING POST-PRODUCTION

In addition to his approach to **pre-visualization**, or the work that goes into a photograph before it is taken, James Van Der Zee was also known as a master of post-production. His techniques included retouching on negatives, **hand-coloring** prints, and the printing of multiple images on one print to create **photomontages**. These skills are another example of how technology shapes the way an artist works; Van Der Zee's vision would not have been the same had a photo-editing program like Photoshop been available. Photography was completely manual and, as such, he could only manipulate photos as far as the deftness and sensitivity of his hands would allow.

Photo retouching became a cherished part of the process for Van Der Zee because it afforded him complete control over the final image. He could get the "faces right," something he was never able to do through drawing or painting. A master of his craft, he learned there were successful, and unsuccessful, ways to retouch a photograph:

> You can see what lines aren't necessary, and you know if you are making a certain type of face what lines to put in there. Some [photographers] would take out *all* the lines and the faces would look just like billiard balls. If it wasn't beautiful, why, I took out the unbeautifulness, put them in the position that they looked beautiful, took out the defects, pulled out all those sagging muscles. Some of them looked like they were worried a lot. I'd pencil them up, take out some of those wrinkles and lines, soften the eyes if they were hard. If they had cross-eyes, I'd straighten them out. If they had gold teeth I could lighten them up. Hair was thin, I'd thicken it, restyle it sometimes.

Today, photo retouching carries with it negative connotations; programs like Photoshop can be used to create blemish-free celebrities, disproportionate and sickly thin models, and otherwise distort the public's perception of natural beauty. However, these

James Van Der Zee, *Do Tell*, 1930. This hand-tinted photograph shows off Van Der Zee's skills as a photo-colorer.

debates did not exist until much later in Van Der Zee's career and even then he was completely unaware.

Regardless, this dialogue wouldn't have changed his mind—he was a determined artist with a vision. Historians and artists alike can still appreciate his approach, regardless of modern contexts. Additionally, his photographs were never a part of this debate because his approach to retouching was responsible and his intent was artistic, not commercial. To Van Der Zee, he was bringing out the best in people: "I put my heart and soul into [my photos] and tried to see that every picture was better looking than the person—if it wasn't better looking than the person talking, then I wasn't satisfied with it."

He rarely had customers who disliked his retouching. He remembered one instance: "I do recall one girl saying, 'Can't you make no pictures that look like me? I'd hate for people to say they were nice pictures but I don't look like that.' I said I could make such pictures and showed her the proofs. 'But the proofs look so *bad*,' she said."

FURTHER TECHNIQUES

Van Der Zee was also a master of hand-coloring photographs. This technique was created before the advent of color photography in order to heighten realism. Artists would apply watercolor, oil paint, or other types of dye to a black-and-white print using a brush, fingers, or even airbrushes. This was a delicate process: if you added too much color you could risk destroying the photo or making the models look garish. Van Der Zee often colored multiple prints of a single image, allowing the client to pick and choose their favorites. He chose paint based on the needs of the image, using watercolors for sheer fabric or dresses while using oils for opaque objects. Curator Westerbeck remarks, "You get the impression that painting directly on a print ... engaged him at least as much as taking the picture in the first place."

All the additional touches added to his photographs came from his own desire to create. Most commercial photographers, as he had learned from his first employer in New Jersey, were content to snap a photo and move along. As Haskins describes, Van Der Zee was different: "Because he considered himself an artist, he took the trouble he did out of pride. But if he had not cared about his subjects, his photographs would have not been as successful, no matter how skillfully he employed light and shade or wielded his etching knife and retouching pencil."

USING THE PHOTOMONTAGE

The last technique Van Der Zee was well known for was his ability to create illusionistic, fantastical, and even ghostly photomontages. A photomontage is any composite of two or more photographs. There are infinite ways to combine multiple images; from literally cutting and pasting parts together to using digital software to seamlessly integrate disparate pieces. Before the advent of digital photography, Van Der Zee and other photographers combined images either on the film itself or in the printing process.

One way to create an image in-camera was to take a **double exposure**. This involved shooting an image on film, rewinding the film, and shooting another image over it. Double exposures created ghostly overlays, but made it hard to anticipate exactly how the two images would interact beforehand. While this would prove exciting for artists like the Dadaists or Surrealists, who left compositions up to chance, this would not be Van Der Zee's working process.

For artists who sought a more controlled process of making photomontages, the darkroom was the place to be. One technique would expose multiple negatives on a single print. An artist could block out the areas they didn't want to print ahead of time, exposing parts of images like puzzle pieces onto the print. To add more control, the artist could **dodge**, decrease exposure time

A GLIMPSE INTO THE AFTERLIFE

Science-fiction writer Arthur C. Clark once said, "Any sufficiently advanced technology is indistinguishable from magic." This is how photography became the championed medium of the Spiritualist movement in the nineteenth and twentieth centuries. **Spiritualism** is the belief that spirits of the dead can communicate with the living in order to impart otherworldly wisdom. At the movement's peak, from roughly the 1840s to the 1920s, it was projected to have more than eight million followers in the United States and Europe. Even Sir Arthur Conan Doyle, writer of the logical Sherlock Holmes stories, was a devoted follower. Mediums performed séances and other feats as a way to convince spectators of the afterlife, but with the advent of photography they now had the means to show it. In 1861, amateur photographer William Mumler took a self-portrait that, when developed, revealed a ghostly face. After examining the image, he realized it had been a double exposure. He began working as a medium, charging high prices for his photographs. Mumler was eventually discovered as a fraud when he began inserting living people's likenesses into his photos. Regardless of truth, the magic had caught on. **Spirit photography** had spread the gospel of Spiritualism. Though modernized, these beliefs and practices are still in use, proving that while technology may change, our fascination with the afterlife will not.

Houdini and the ghost of Abraham Lincoln, circa 1920–1930. Houdini, the famous stage magician, was a staunch advocate against Spiritualism. This photograph, with its absurd inclusion of Abraham Lincoln, was intended to show how easily Spiritualist photography could be faked.

in one area to make it lighter, or **burn**, increase exposure time in one area to make it darker, as needed. This was the technique most often employed by Van Der Zee.

It's no surprise Van Der Zee arrived at this technique since it was a favorite with Victorian photographers. They designed amusing postcards and comics depicting "strange or impossible creatures," figures with "the wrong head stuck on a different body," and other fantasies. Early Spiritualists and ghost hunters would latch onto the photomontage in order to prove existence of mystical or otherworldly beings. Van Der Zee, however, would use it for both practical and artistic purposes.

Van Der Zee utilized the photomontage in many striking ways. By the 1940s, he had developed a method to insert more elaborate backdrops into portraits, a "labor-saving device that kept him from having to repeat every conceivable pose against all options for backgrounds." Similarly, he would often use props to serve as placeholders for elements he would incorporate later: "A cutout of a cocker spaniel … might be a surrogate for a hunting dog in a picture of a woman wearing a riding habit."

But he didn't just use the technique for functional reasons. Artistically, Van Der Zee found he could create compelling narratives through the use of photographic overlays. One of his most famous photographs, *Future Expectations*, depicts a seated young bride holding her bouquet, with her proud groom standing beside her. He looks down at her, top hat in hand, while she faces the camera. They are in a beautifully painted set made to look like a grand parlor. But the most striking part of the image is that which is not physically there: Sitting on the floor below is an ethereal image of a young girl playing with a baby doll. Superimposed onto the print, this image was meant to embody the hope, joy, and a family plan the couple has for the future.

Van Der Zee also combined multiple images in his calendar photos and shots of children. The stories these images told ran from fun to sentimental to contemplative. In an iconic photo entitled *His Pipe*, Van Der Zee inserts a wisp of white smoke billowing up from an unattended smoking pipe. At the top of the photo, the smoke opens to a vignette of a woman seated at a piano. This second image is titled *Her Cigarette*. Is this the woman

James Van Der Zee, *Future Expectations*, 1926. The most famous example of Van Der Zee's photomontage technique, this image utilized an ethereal superimposition of a child to imply future domestic bliss.

The Artist's and the Camera's Eye

the smoker was thinking of? Or is this the woman he neglected in order to smoke a pipe with friends? These were the types of questions and stories Van Der Zee liked to imply.

Many of his soldier portraits incorporate collaged imagery as well. The photo *Memories* depicts an elderly veteran sitting in a chair, brooding. The room is shrouded in dark shadows, save for the few pops of light on the set and the American flag behind him. Following the man's eyes, we are led to the ghostly overlay of soldiers fighting, most likely taken from a painting, illustration, or stock photo. The former soldier has been caught "in a moment of remembrance of his lost comrades-in-arms." The effect is pensive and thoughtful, if not a little otherworldly.

FUNERAL PHOTOGRAPHY

The most alluring and powerful use of the photomontage in Van Der Zee's work can be seen in his funerary images. These images are instantly striking—they both repel and attract the viewer at the same time. Postmortem photography, or portraits of the recently deceased, was a common practice at the time. These photos were a crucial part of the mourning process for many families: "In some cases, especially when it came to very young children, a funerary portrait would be the only photograph ever taken of a person, and the only photograph their families would have to remember them. For people who had migrated to Harlem, funerary portraits could be sent back to relatives they had left behind who could not attend a loved one's funeral."

The deceased would be photographed at their funeral, in their coffin, or sometimes even staged with other family members so as to appear alive. While the modern eye may think these images morbid, at the time these cherished mementos were a reminder of loved ones lost.

Van Der Zee did his best to soften the painful nature of these photos by imbuing them with beauty. Through the use of montage he would add poetry, biblical scriptures, and angelic imagery to surround and support the deceased. The final images were exquisite; each photograph ornamental yet simplistic, peaceful yet emotionally stirring. When asked why he added inserts into his death portraits, he responded, "I just put them in to take away from the gruesomeness of the pictures, to make it more like 'suffering little children to come unto me and I'll give you rest.'"

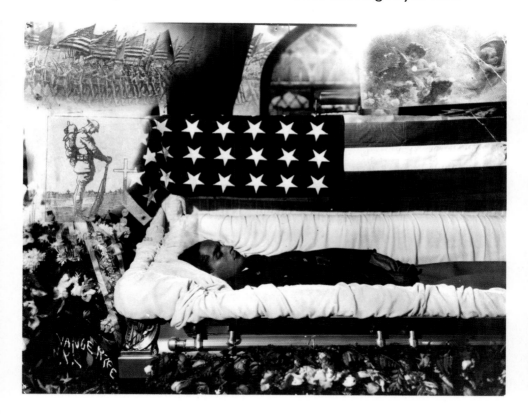

James Van Der Zee, *The Last Good-bye, Overseas*, 1941. Van Der Zee's funerary portraits used photomontage to humanize the decreased—images of soldiers honored the man's military service while angelic imagery offered a gesture of blessing and peace.

In certain cases, if Van Der Zee had photographed the deceased in both life and death, he would use both images in the final funerary portrait. His two most famous examples of this are from the funerals of Blanche Powell and his daughter, Rachel.

In Powell's funerary portrait, we see her casket glowing white, made small by the grandeur of the gothic church and the amount of attendees. A choir sings on the upper balcony level, and floating about the procession is an image of young Blanche holding a parasol.

Rachel Van Der Zee's funerary portrait is more intimate, the young girl's stunning profile surrounded in glowing white fabric and flowers. Above her is the likeness of Jesus, softly touching her funerary wreath. Below that is the vaporous profile of Rachel, wearing a white button-up or possibly a choir uniform. She stares steadfastly ahead, looking slightly upwards. Through this perfect marriage of images, Rachel's live portrait is transfigured into an angelic one, her eyes staring toward the heavens above. Beside that is a small poem with verses about farewells and twilight.

THE HARLEM BOOK OF THE DEAD

The only artist's book Van Der Zee ever produced was of his funeral portraits. Entitled *The Harlem Book of the Dead*, it was published as a limited edition monograph. The book featured eighteen stunning reproductions of funerary photographs, paired with Owen Dodson's poetry and interviews between the artist and Camille Billops. Page layouts incorporated art deco–inspired filigree: sleek borders that invoke the style and design sensibility of the 1920s. On the dust jacket appears a succinct synopsis: "*The Harlem Book of the Dead* with its photographs, poems, and text are more than representational reflections of mourning rites. They reveal the history of a time in Harlem, now past, when society cared for both the living and the dead, the belief that we must preserve a standard of pride representing order high in spiritual

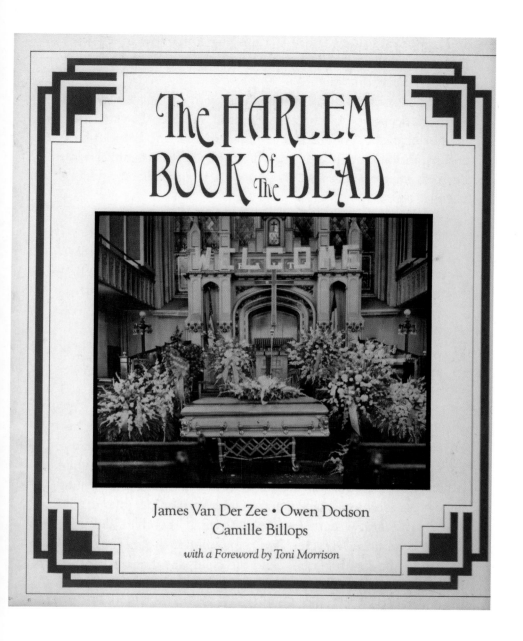

The HARLEM
BOOK of the DEAD

James Van Der Zee • Owen Dodson
Camille Billops

with a Foreword by Toni Morrison

The cover for *The Harlem Book of the Dead*, a collection of Van Der Zee funerary images set against interviews and poetry, features his photo *Welcome*, circa 1930.

and temporal values. There is a purging of sorrow in the very pageantry of funerals. Carelessness about death might reflect carelessness about life."

The back of the book includes a list with each plate alongside a description given by the artist himself. Van Der Zee's written memories of the funerals and circumstances are sometimes hazy and sometimes tragic, but regardless, his images resonate with deep care and compassion. One image is accompanied by a more peculiar story:

> She was … shot by her sweetheart at a party with a noiseless gun. She complained of being sick at the party and friends said, "Well, why don't you lay down?" and they taken her in the room and laid her down. After they undressed her and loosened her clothes, they saw the blood on her dress. They asked her about it and she said, "I'll tell you tomorrow, yes, I'll tell you tomorrow." She was just trying to give him a chance to get away. For the picture, I placed flowers on her chest.

Some are brief—"She wanted her picture taken with her husband on the day of the funeral. I don't remember her name, except that she was a taxi driver with her own cab."—while other photos are heartbreaking. Plate 8 depicts a seated young father, dressed in a black tie and suit, holding his infant child before a funeral wreath. He looks down at the child with love and consideration. Van Der Zee remembered the tragedy: "The reason for having the father hold the child was that the mother was sick in the hospital and couldn't get out. The child died in the meantime. If it wasn't for the picture, the mother wouldn't have seen the child for the last time."

The Harlem Book of the Dead is a powerful work of art. While only a crosshair of Van Der Zee's portfolio, his funeral images get to the heart of his artistic voice. He was an early photographer, influenced by changing technology and adept at manual processes. He was also an uncompromising artist, working unaware of artistic movements and loyal to his own vision. Above all, he was a master at his medium, using photography to tell beautiful stories and create powerful images. Mia Tramz, associate photo editor at *Time* magazine, describes the impact of *The Harlem Book of the Dead* and Van Der Zee's work at large: "The book is an ode not only to lives past, but to a time past—and to a slice of history that might otherwise be lost. It is a meditation on death and loss, but also on beauty. In the book, and in his work, VanDerZee was not only a photographer, but a custodian of memory."

CHAPTER FIVE

RE-ENVISIONING BLACK CULTURE

James Van Der Zee will forever be remembered as the "Eyes of Harlem." The 1973 *Black Photographer's Annual* wrote he was "best known for his capturing and preserving the pictorial history of Harlem USA during the first half of the twentieth century." It is unanimously recognized that Van Der Zee's work presented a wealth of invaluable knowledge about life in the first half of the twentieth century. What is discussed in greater detail is what these photographs mean in the context of African-American history. This debate begins with the cultural, social, and artistic movements of the Harlem Renaissance.

THE HARLEM RENAISSANCE AND THE NEW NEGRO

The Harlem Renaissance spanned from approximately 1920 to 1935. It coincided with two important migrations of the black community: the geographical movements of the **Great Migration**

Opposite: James Van Der Zee, *Guarantee Photo Studio*, 1917.

and the influx of people specifically moving into Harlem. The first Great Migration lasted from 1910 to 1930. During that time, over 1.6 million Southern black workers headed north toward newly industrialized cities. These booming cities promised good wages, decent housing, and an American ideal of a happy homestead. Author Henry Louis Gates Jr. describes this time of change:

> African Americans reinvented themselves, as more than a million souls removed themselves from the provinces to the metropole, from the periphery to the center, from the South to the North, from the agricultural to the urban, from the nineteenth century to the twentieth. The greatest transformation of all … [was] the outcome of the exchange of traditional Southern and Northern black cultures and the resulting synthesis of the two.

In New York City, Harlem also experienced a wave of new arrivals. Jervis Anderson, the author of *This Was Harlem*, said that "almost all blacks once dreamed of coming [north]—in search of refuge, opportunity, gaiety, an idea of freedom and a brighter future." This sense of progress, just by moving and asserting control over the future of one's life, began to fuel a confidence in the African-American community.

In 1917, the United States entered World War I. War often accelerates philosophy and culture because it forces people to reevaluate our place in society and society's place in the world, and to contemplate the value of life and death. The first truly global war, World War I ignited an abundance of new ideas that spread through both white and black communities. The concept of "Newness" was one of these ideas. It encompassed thoughts on everything from science to psychology to women's rights to humanism to morality. A new archetype began to develop in the minds of American culture: the **New Negro**.

James Van Der Zee, *Lady at the Piano*, 1941. Well dressed, well learned, and talented, this woman embodied the ideals of the "New Negro."

Re-Envisioning Black Culture   **87**

When this term was first coined in the *Cleveland Gazette* in 1895 there were conflicting interpretations of what it meant. Scholar Henry Louis Gates Jr. wrote: "The New Negro was a paradoxical metaphor that combined a concern with history and culture antecedents with a deep concern for an articulated racial heritage. [This concept] would establish, once and for all, the highly public faces of a once-subjugated, but now proud, race."

On the one hand, both the New Negro and the Harlem Renaissance existed partly because the white community had begun to acknowledge the achievements of black Americans. Black creatives and visionaries had always existed, but it wasn't until this time that the white community actively patronized and engaged with this demographic. Mainstream publishers began putting out an unprecedented number of books by black authors, charitable foundations began supporting prizes for black artists, and jazz musicians were beloved and praised by all people. However, as Haskins describes, little had really changed: "The Negro was just the same as he had always been. Any newness he had acquired was within the new eyes with which whites viewed him."

Regardless of its accuracy, both the ideal of the New Negro and the Harlem Renaissance, at the time termed the New Negro Movement, allowed black Americans to assert new identities that could be accepted by the mass culture. Historian Cheryl Wall writes: "The New Negro consciousness resulted from an attempt, fairly successful on the whole, to convert a defensive into an offensive position, a handicap into an incentive."

Photography was a part of this new assertion. Before and during the turn of the century, Victorian photo traditions had proliferated stereotypical depictions of black men, women, and children. Caricatures, manipulated photography, and even pseudoscience aimed to make fun of and degrade the black race in popular culture. These images did not describe the African-American experience and so, with the added tools of the photographer, artists worked to proliferate an image of their heritage that was their own. Author Deborah Willis elaborates on this:

> There was a concerted effort to find the "self" in visual images. Photographs made by black studio photographers during this period reveal both the creation of the photographer and the self-image projected by the sitter … By exploring the New Negro through text and images, black Americans offered a new paradigm through which to explore the significance of the photographic image and … to transform the mythos projected on black communities by the larger society.

Photography as a medium has often been mistaken as a literal representation of life. We know this to not be true; a photograph can be manipulated, composed, or altered to fit an artist's vision. Still, we take the photographs as a "type of guarantee, a visual proof, of an object's or person's presence at a specific moment." In this way, photography actually helped to counter the traditional representations of African Americans. These images would serve as proof that black Americans were as "multidimensional as everyone else."

Van Der Zee's images "offer a different kind of evidence of black and American possibility," contrary to the "common images of black Americans—downtrodden rural or urban citizens." There are a few reasons for this, the most plentiful being his representation of the emerging black middle class. Author Miriam Thaggert describes Van Der Zee's photos as "overtly, aggressively middle class," citing how this "middle-class status is most evident" in his various compositions.

James Van Der Zee, *Cousin Susan Porter, Harlem*, 1915. This iconic image of Van Der Zee's cousin embodies the black socialites who enjoyed a comfortable life in Harlem during the early part of the twentieth century.

EXAMINING VAN DER ZEE'S WORK

Van Der Zee's work was varied. For instance, the photos *Harlem Socialites Taking Afternoon Tea* and *Cousin Susan Porter, Harlem,* put forth an idea of refined and comfortable living. A sense of pride and achievement appear in his school, church, and civic photos. The photos of parades and marches exude "optimism, a belief in the power of peaceful protest." Much like the artist himself, Van Der Zee's photos show Harlem and its residents as happy people. They were hardworking and socially engaged. When they faced tragedy, they faced it together. Van Der Zee's funerary photographs "reflect the communal significance of African-American spirituality and the concept that the deceased is ever present in the daily activities of the living." Throughout all these photographs, we see a close-knit community that nourishes itself from the inside and seeks to accomplish more. Thaggert points out that, "Even in 'casual' or presumably spontaneous photographs there is a suggestion of upward mobility."

It wasn't just middle-class clients who projected this sense of honor. As an artist, Van Der Zee himself actively fashioned his photos to tell the stories he wanted. By reimagining ordinary models into something grander, he could depict his subjects as heroic, self-aware, and beautiful. There is an exciting "tension between biography and fiction" in these portraits. The scenes may at times appear artificial and formal, but always the subjects featured communicate a sense of honesty and real emotion. Van Der Zee utilized the familiarity and respectability of the Victorian photograph to tell a new story, that of the proud black American. Deborah Wills describes it as an ingenious approach: "His use of nineteenth-century formalist compositional elements to photograph twentieth-century subjects was an elegant and intelligent way of devising a revisionist and optimistic overview of the African-American experience."

A CRITICAL APPROACH

There are some, however, who criticize Van Der Zee's approach. Van Der Zee's work is deeply ensconced in classical photography. His images, regardless of their message, were created from within a system that favored traditional standards of quality and taste. Much like the New Negro, which arose as a way to define the black community to outsiders, this type of reading of Van Der Zee's work implies that he and other black photographers require validation from the dominant white culture. Roland Barthes, author of *Camera Lucida*, described these flaws inherent in Van Der Zee's approach through a portrait of a black family: "I am sympathetically interested, as a docile culture subject, in what the photograph has to say, for it speaks (it is a "good" photograph): it utters respectability, family life, conformism, Sunday best. An effort of social advancement in order to assume the White man's attributes (an effort touching by reason of it's naiveté)."

Others have noted Van Der Zee's conformity to conservative pictorial traditions. Hilton Als, in his introductory essay to the exhibition catalogue for *James Van Der Zee: Harlem Guaranteed*, writes about a childhood figure. This older neighborhood girl pronounced her strong African identity by denouncing anything that was an extension of white culture. Als likens Van Der Zee's approach as an incarnation of white culture; it used a language devised by white photographers to describe white experience. However, as Als's story progresses, we discover that this girl was more talk than action. Her lifestyle publically displayed contradictions, and in the end, she denies that she had ever declared herself completely sovereign from the culture at large. Als appears to suggest that, while it would be ideal to invent a new mode of expression outside the white tradition, such a thing is difficult to put into practice. His final reading of Van Der Zee's work softens, implying that despite the photographer's imperfect vessel, his messages came through with conviction.

FOLK, NAÏVE, AND VISIONARY ART

Art critic Ben Lifson writes, "James Van Der Zee is one of the purest examples in photography of what we … call a folk, popular, primitive, or naïve artist—one who works intuitively without a thought for the larger world of art or for his place in history of his chosen medium." But was James Van Der Zee really a **folk artist**? People who don't define themselves as "fine artists," such as indigenous people and common tradesmen, are folk artists. Their work is often utilitarian or decorative, and their skills are acquired through community tradition or apprenticeship. Examples would be Hopi Native Americans making Kachina dolls, sailors making macramé, and the Amish making hex signs. **Naïve or primitive art** refers to work that appears simplistic or childlike. This does not mean it was created by an untrained artist. Famous painters like Picasso and Henri Rousseau worked in this style, citing folk art from Africa and Central America as influences. The term can be considered pejorative; it suggests a lack of quality and implies that influences, like folk art, are less valuable than "fine art." **Visionary art** is art produced by "self-taught individuals, usually without formal training, whose works arise from an innate personal vision that revels foremost in the creative act itself." Van Der Zee's work can fit in all, or none, of these categories, leaving his work to be defined by the viewers themselves.

James Van Der Zee, *The Fisherman's Club*, 1928. Civic, social, and fraternal clubs were an important part of Harlem life. Here, Van Der Zee captures the honor and camaraderie shared by the members of this organization.

These debates are deeply ensconced in **postmodernism**, a mode of thinking that did not emerge until the late twentieth century. Considering the historical context, and the fact that the artist was politically indifferent, James Van Der Zee's work is rarely the subject of intense criticism. Curator Colin Westerbeck describes how most people view the photographer's work and creative aspirations: "Van Der Zee was indeed a documentarian. He was making a record of the way his subjects actually lived. And even when he wasn't doing so, he was at least documenting aspirations to which those subjects were legitimately entitled. If he had not made his photographs and, just as importantly, taken care to preserve them as best he could even when he was in desperate circumstances, our sense of African American history would be greatly diminished."

As an artist, Van Der Zee remained neutral toward his subjects' lives. He was a photographer by profession and had a commitment to his clients not to align his personal politics with his photos (although he took artistic license freely). Cecil Beaton, an English photographer, noted Van Der Zee was called upon in Harlem to "capture the tragedy as well as the happiness in life, turning his camera on death and marriage with the same detachment." *New York Times* author Margo Jefferson describes this as the photographer's ability to "capture all the shades and ambiguities that lie between tragedy and happiness." James Van Der Zee did not apply a modernist thesis to all his work, but instead he became a conduit through which the personalities and lives of his subjects were expressed.

Van Der Zee, while not world famous before 1969, was well known as a respected photographer while in Harlem. It is because of this good reputation that he was contacted by Marcus Garvey to be his official photographer.

MARCUS GARVEY

Marcus Mosiah Garvey was born in Jamaica in 1887. As a young man he was passionate about activism and participated in unions, formed political clubs, and started newspapers. He traveled to Central and South America, documenting the plight of mining and plantation workers. He even moved to London to study ancient African history and write for the *African Times and Orient Review*. Through these experiences, it became clear to him that, without organization or government support, his people would continue to suffer.

In 1914, he returned to Jamaica to form the Universal Negro Improvement Association (UNIA). The UNIA believed in **Pan-Africanism**, or the solidarity between people of African descent, and promoted Black Nationalism, a movement to create an independent, self-governing, black nation. In 1916, Garvey moved to Harlem and formed an American branch. He established *the Negro World* newspaper and the Black Star Line, a steamship company that carried African produce to the United States and aimed to offer passage back to African for African Americans. His most

James Van Der Zee, *Garvey's Women's Brigade*, 1924. Garvey's Auxiliary Corps were just one of the ways women could participate in Black Nationalism, performing at parades and peaceful protests.

astounding achievement was to organize the First International Convention of Negro Peoples of the World in Madison Square Garden in 1920. For the first time, people of African descent came from different countries around the globe to discuss social, economic, and political conditions.

Despite his positive achievements, Garvey began receiving backlash for failed projects. The Black Star Line had been besieged with problems from the beginning. Unsafe vessels, overstocked ships, rotting cargo, employee thievery, and even sabotage caused by agents of the US government had sent the enterprise spiraling. However, the biggest tarnish on Marcus Garvey's record was when in 1922 he met with Ku Klux Klan leaders in Atlanta, Georgia. Garvey was in trouble: "W. E. B. Du Bois immediately ran a series of scathing editorials in the *Crisis*, while other black writers—pan-Africanists, socialists, and Marxists, formerly UNIA sympathizers—now turned against a beleaguered Marcus Garvey. Suffering such great loss of face in the black community was severely damaging." The final blow was in 1923 when he was charged with mail fraud based on a brochure that misrepresented the Black Star Line's vessel.

Marcus Garvey began to revise his approach. He had lost his credibility; members of the black and white communities viewed him as a **charlatan**, or fraud. He needed a revised public persona that was refined, orderly, and softened his radical approach. Miriam Thaggert wrote that Van Der Zee's photographs invoked a "sense of normalcy that borders on the banal and a correctness that makes them conventional." It was this conventionality that Garvey needed so badly. In 1924, while Garvey was awaiting sentencing, Van Der Zee signed a contract to become the official photographer of the UNIA.

Bringing on Van Der Zee was the first part of a "design to retrieve some vestige of the grandeur Garvey had once enjoyed but has since lost." His photographic style, steeped in "secure, middle-class, genteel traditions," immediately linked the sitter with the "established emblems of wealth and high social rank." These were the visual ideals Garvey wanted associated with the UNIA.

He began to advocate the "Gospel of Success," an ideology that, through hard work and perseverance, racial independence would come. This "gospel" was modeled after the American dream. Garvey had completely changed his tactics: "For Garvey, even when the language was radical, the underlying ethos was **bourgeois**. In 1924, he was asserting that one road to black equality with the other races of the world was the replication of the core institutions of modern [i.e., European] nation states. James Van Der Zee's portraiture represented the epitome of Harlem petit bourgeois values."

WORKING WITH GARVEY

Van Der Zee began taking photos of UNIA parades and auxiliary drill exercises, studio portraits of members and their families, and photos of Garvey with high-ranking local officials. These last images were widely publicized as a means of positive propaganda for the cause. Van Der Zee also photographed the Fourth International Convention, framing Garvey in some of his most iconic moments. He appears as a commanding political figure: riding down city streets in a chauffeured limousine, in his most resplendent regalia, surrounded by cheering crowds and parade-goers with signs.

Upon the conclusion of the convention, Van Der Zee was inundated with work. He received requests from not only those who participated in the events but from UNIA members worldwide. Van Der Zee chose twelve of the best images from the year and prepared a 1925 calendar. Unfortunately, Garvey would not be able to enjoy it: in 1925 he was incarcerated for mail fraud until his release and deportation in 1927.

PHOTOS WITH POWER

What Garvey recognized, as well as the other historians who have examined Van Der Zee's work, is that the photograph has the power "to become its own truth." Roger C. Birt described the power of the black photographer in the early twentieth century: "In a society and at a time where a black man was considered dangerous for daring to claim that black was beautiful (or handsome), the ... photographer set out to provide a legacy that challenged the prevalent stereotypes of black men and women."

CHAPTER SIX

VAN DER ZEE'S LEGACY

The legacy of James Van Der Zee has not diminished since his death. In 1984, New York City Mayor Ed Koch declared an official James Van Der Zee Week. This announcement coincided with a show mounted at the City Gallery of New York that featured twenty vintage prints, fifteen portraits made within three years of his death, and personal memorabilia from his Harlem home. Bess Myerson, the Cultural Affairs Commissioner, said, "James Van Der Zee has given us his eyes and his heart and his soul, and we are transported into lives that are so real."

This was the first of countless exhibitions that the artist would participate in posthumously. His work has been collected and shown at internationally renowned museums such as the Metropolitan Museum of Art, the Museum of Modern Art, the International Center for Photography, the National Gallery of Art, the Alternative Center for International Art, the Art Institute of Chicago, and countless others.

James Van Der Zee, *Intrigue*, 1935.

MORE MODERN REMEMBRANCES

In 1993, the National Portrait Gallery in Washington, DC, organized an impressive retrospective of his work entitled *James Van Der Zee: Photographer 1886–1983*. The accompanying book, published under the same name, included Deborah Willis-Braithwaite's writing on the historical importance of the artist's work, even if only after the fact: "[Van Der Zee's work] was not known to the generation of photographers that came of age after the 1940s, for whom it might have made a difference. His secure, middle-class upbringing gave him an invaluable perspective on African-American life and culture, enabling him to make photographs that were removed from what came to be, by the Depression, the predominant and accepted way of depicting the African-American experience in photographs."

In 2002, the Michael Rosenfield Gallery of Art curated the show *James Van Der Zee: Harlem Guaranteed*, which included thirty rare prints of the artist's work and a beautifully designed catalogue. The *New York Times* hailed the exhibition as "small but dynamic," and his work was praised as capturing the "intellectual lights of the Harlem Renaissance." The show was aptly paired against another exhibition, *Colored: Consider the Rainbow*, by artist Betye Saar. Her autobiographical collages, made from old photographs, served as a contemporary reflection on how memories are both distilled and distorted through photographic material.

In 2004, the Art Institute of Chicago mounted an exhibition entitled *The James Van Der Zee Studio*, and published a catalogue that featured an essay by curator Colin Westerbeck and artist Dawoud Bey. The show featured some rare examples of the artist's hand-colored prints as well as multiples of the same model with different, super-imposed backgrounds. These works provided a rare glimpse into James Van Der Zee's process and photographic skills. Westerbeck wrote on the triumph of the artist's work:

"Van Der Zee's portraits are about dreams, or rather, about that special time in Harlem when dreams and realities might actually meet in the lives of middle-class African Americans."

Van Der Zee's first solo exhibition in Canada was at the Wedge Gallery in Toronto in 1999, organized because the gallery owner had a personal connection to the work. Ken Montague had attended the infamous *Harlem On My Mind* exhibition at the Metropolitan Museum of Art. "I couldn't have been more than six or seven," he said, "and yet those images have stuck with me." Maia Sutnik, the curator of photography at the Art Gallery of Ontario at the time, described James Van Der Zee's impact: "His work has deep context, but the context is meaningless unless you have a consummate artist who can convey his vision to an audience. Van Der Zee's is enormously compelling material."

WORKS REVISITED AND REVITALIZED

The absorbing qualities of Van Der Zee's artistry have allowed his work to be framed and revisited in a surprising variety of contexts. His photographs are included in curated shows whose themes range from the Harlem Renaissance to the more abstract concepts. In 2014, the Madison Museum of Contemporary Art in Wisconsin presented *Turn Turn Turn*, a group show "inspired by the lyrical language of Ecclesiastes 3, which meditates on the circular nature of time as reflected in the seasons."

The Studio Museum in Harlem has passionately kept Van Der Zee's work relevant and engaged with new audiences. In 2005, Van Der Zee was included in *hrlm: pictures*, which featured the work of twenty-seven artists. The 2010 exhibition *Inside the Collection: Interiors from the Studio Museum* highlighted some of Van Der Zee's rarely seen images of Harlem apartments. *Who, What, Wear: Selections from the Permanent Collection*, mounted in 2011, explored the evolution of African-American style and fashion.

INSPIRING OTHERS

In addition to exhibitions, the Studio Museum provides educational programs inspired by Van Der Zee's work. Their monthly calendar boasts a plethora of workshops for families and children on topics of photo collage, historical photography, and themes of community. Their most ambitious program, Expanding the Walls, has occurred annually since 2001: "*Expanding the Walls: Making Connections Between Photography, History and Community* ... is an eight-month residency in which New York–area high school students explore the history and techniques of photography. Through experimentation, discussion, gallery visits and workshops led by contemporary artists, the students build community as each explores and defines his or her art practice ... The James Van Der Zee Archives—housed at the Studio Museum in Harlem—have been the primary catalyst for the students' critical reflections on the representation of culture and community."

By inviting the next generation of artists and thinkers to interact with Van Der Zee's photography and the history it represents, the Studio Museum is keeping his legacy alive in a powerful way. These efforts help educate youth on African-American history, encourage new ways of connecting with the past, and bolster creativity.

INFLUENCING CONTEMPORARIES

Many contemporary artists have cited James Van Der Zee as an inspiration, including photographer Dawoud Bey. Born in 1953 and raised in Queens, New York, Bey was always interested in his family's history in Harlem. At the age of sixteen, intrigued more by the controversy than the art, he went to the Metropolitan Museum of Art to see what *Harlem On My Mind* was all about. To his surprise, he did not find a single protestor in sight. With no other real option, he decided to go in and see the exhibition. He was in awe of what he found: "While others addressed the various triumphs and pitfalls in the formation and evolution of the Harlem

Dawoud Bey's *A Boy Eating a Foxy Pop* was displayed at the nineteenth Paris Photo Fair in 2015.

community, Van Der Zee's photographs spoke to me in a more subdued voice. They simply bore witness to the men, women, and children who had, with a quiet dignity and profound ordinariness, populated this community in the twenties, thirties, and forties."

Bey found these images so powerful, partly because they were completely foreign to him: "What was so striking to me at the time was how little resemblance these pictures bore to the image of Harlem that even I, growing up in the black middle-class suburbs of Queens, New York, had come to imagine. Van Der Zee's photographs became for me, at that moment, a wonderful window through which an unseen past and a largely unseen black subject were made vividly and immediately accessible."

It was then that Bey began taking photos of his own. From 1975 to 1979 he created a series of photographs entitled *Harlem, USA*. On an almost weekly basis he visited Harlem and took images of its residents. These photographs depicted a very different Harlem than the one Van Der Zee knew. However, both artists captured the neighborhood during a time of great change and used their lenses to capture the beauty, pride, and personality in their subjects. Not all of the Harlem natives featured in Bey's images were as optimistic as Van Der Zee's, but they were honest with the camera. Today, Dawoud Bey is renowned for his images of black and marginalized communities and continues to exhibit his work at museums across the country.

Other artists have also taken up the charge of documenting Harlem. One such artist, Alix Dejean, has been working underground since the 1970s. Born in Haiti to a wealthy family, Dejean moved to Bushwich, Brooklyn, in 1965. He studied civil engineering at City College but picked up photography as a hobby when he started attending jazz performances in the Village. In the early 1970s he met Frankie Crocker, a well-known radio DJ, who introduced him to the music scene. He would go on to photograph artists like James Brown and the Jackson Five, as well as celebrities like Stevie Wonder, Don King, Mike Tyson, Al Sharpton, and Congressman Charles B. Rangel.

He became interested in Harlem after photographing at Leviticus, a popular Midtown disco. The drug kingpins Leroy Nicholas Barnes and Frank Lucas hired him to take pictures of their lavish parties. Dejean explains: "When I first met them I didn't know what they did, but I photographed them as real people, complex people."

The more time he spent in Harlem, the more his reputation grew. Soon, he was known as "Alley Cat," because of his constant prowl for photographic subjects. He photographed people on the streets, at barbershops, in the park, and on brownstone stoops. Thousands of these images are archived in his Brooklyn apartment, but their real homes are in the hands of his subjects. He sells prints for about twenty dollars, though the price is negotiable. While his works "have never been publically exhibited, they are prized by Harlem residents, tucked in family albums and in the frames on apartment walls." Jeff Terry, a returning customer, describes Dejean's character: "Alix is a legend. He's the hood photographer, a real street celebrity."

Artist Dawoud Bey in 2011.

Youths in Harlem in 1986, as photographed by Alix Dejean.

Much like Van Der Zee, Dejean is largely self-taught. Also like Van Der Zee, Dejean does not create work to be exhibited as "fine art," but instead takes photos so that his subjects may enjoy them. He, too, has seen "all the changing faces of Harlem," from "the emergence of hip-hop to the violent rise of the crack epidemic to its current makeover as a result of gentrification." The most striking similarity between Van Der Zee and Dejean is the role and aim both photographers had in their subjects' lives. Dejean explains, "I'm the people's photographer … I try to capture a beautiful moment in your life."

VAN DER ZEE IN FILM

Filmmakers have been inspired by the legacy of James Van Der Zee, too. His photographs have been displayed in films such as *Idlewild* (2006), *Jumping the Broom* (2011), and *The Manchurian Candidate* (2004). Interestingly, *The Bill Cosby Show* (1984–1992) used one of Van Der Zee's photographs to portray Cosby's father. The 2002 thriller *One Hour Photo*, starring Robin Williams, pays homage to the photographer by naming the character of the detective after him.

In 2014, director Allen Harris, in conjunction with PBS, produced a nonfiction documentary based on the book *Reflections in Black: A History of Black Photographers* by Deborah Willis. This film charted the relatively unknown history of black photography: "The first documentary to explore the role of photography in shaping the identity, aspirations, and social emergence of African Americans from slavery to the present, *Through a Lens Darkly: Black Photographers and the Emergence of a People* probes the recesses of American history through images that have been suppressed, forgotten, and lost."

STAMPED A MASTER OF AMERICAN PHOTOGRAPHY

On June 13, 2002, the United States Postal Service released a commemorative set of stamps titled Masters of American Photography. The collection features twenty different artworks taken by some of the most influential American photographers. It was initially suggested that the stamps feature exclusively the work of Ansel Adams, in honor of the anniversary of the photographer's centennial birthday. However, it was decided that by curating a broader spectrum of work, the collection would better highlight the complex photographic history in America. However, deciding on what images to include was not an easy task. Each year the CSCA, or Citizens' Stamp Advisory Committee, sorts through thousands of stamp suggestions only to choose a handful to produce. Peter C. Bunnell, a photographic historian at Princeton University, assisted in the selection process: "It is an extremely difficult task to bring the whole history of American photography down to twenty photographs," he said. "In most cases where there were comparisons to make, it was a personal choice as to the better or more significant photographer … Also, we were interested in a mix of subjects—portrait, landscape, architecture, still life, etc." James Van Der Zee's iconic portrait *My Corsage* was included in the collection.

The film features the work of Van Der Zee, alongside masters of the medium like Carrie Mae Weems, Lorna Simpson, Anthony Barboza, Hank Willis Thomas, Coco Fusco, Clarissa Sligh, Gordon Parks, and many more. *Through a Lens Darkly* was a project ten years in the making. The research team first collected over fifteen thousand images from communities across America. Then they began touring the Digital Diaspora Family Reunion Roadshow, an interactive community project that encouraged people to "rethink the educational value of their family photo albums through the act of sharing them (and their stories) with … a live audience." Through this active participation the team was able to collect another six thousand images that dated as far back as the 1840s. In the end, the documentary shows 950 images and covers 170 years of American history.

The *New York Times* praised the film for its ambition and scope: "Mr. Harris's film is a family memoir, a tribute to unsung artists and a lyrical, at times heartbroken, meditation on imagery and identity. The film is always absorbing to watch, but only once it's over do you begin to grasp the extent of its ambitions, and just how much it has done within a packed, compact hour and a half."

The most important goal of the film was to provide photographic representations of black history. A seemingly simple aim, Harris describes why it shouldn't be taken lightly:

> Images shape popular culture's view of what "blackness" is and who "black people" are—both in the images that are out there but also those hidden from view. At every critical juncture in the evolution of black Americans … black photographers have been there, showing the ordinary daily lives of a people who have been integral to making America what it is. As Deborah Willis notes, when you subtract the images of black photographers, you also subtract the images of African-American family. It is in this absence that stereotypical images proliferate.

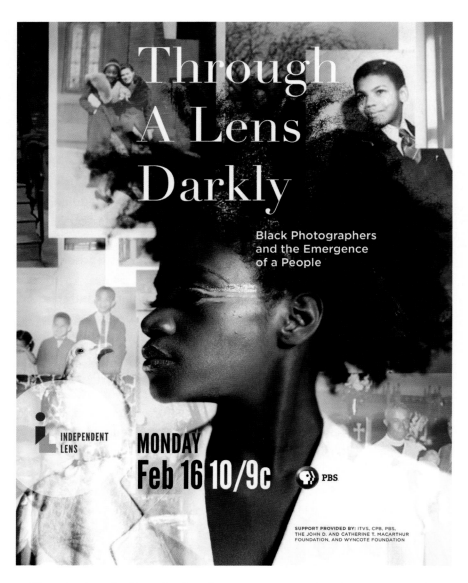

Through a Lens Darkly is the first documentary to explore how photography, both in fine art and family photo albums, defined and continues to transform black identities in America.

A LASTING LEGACY

The dialogue around Van Der Zee's work continues to thrive because of the powerful implications it carries. Historians, artists, filmmakers, and even wedding photographers have sought to understand, contend with, and recreate the themes inherent in his work. He photographed the average person with pride, dignity, and beauty. His portraits allowed us visual access to legends, political figures, and celebrities who will be remembered by history. The shots he took of Harlem life on the streets and in apartments are welcoming and intimate. Van Der Zee's funerary portraits are compelling and otherworldly, utilizing techniques that were advanced for their time. Though the names, dress, and settings are different from the modern world, it is these timeless sentiments that will resonate with viewers today and in the future.

He will be remembered on museum and gallery walls, in beautiful art books, and even on a US stamp. Most of all, he will be remembered for his contributions to American history. Reginald McGhee described it best: "Van Der Zee's works have brought a tremendous amount of warmth, pride, and true insight into the long neglected history of black Americans."

1886 James Augustus Joseph Van Der Zee is born.

1899 Obtains his first camera as a prize for selling ladies' sachet.

1900 Takes his first known photograph, *Trinity Church*.

1905 Moves to New York City.

1907 Marries Kate L. Brown; their daughter Rachel is born; family moves to Phoebus, Virginia; Van Der Zee photographs in Phoebus.

1908 Family moves to New York City and move to Harlem; son Emil is born and by winter dies of pneumonia.

1911 Van Der Zee's older sister, Jennie, opens the Toussaint Conservatory of Art and Music; Van Der Zee takes a job as a photographer's assistant in Newark, New Jersey; John, Charlie, and Mary Van Der Zee die.

1916 Kate leaves Van Der Zee, taking custody of Rachel; meets Gaynella Katz Greenlee while working at the Chatsworth Apartments; Van Der Zee and Gaynella open the Guaranteed Photo Studio in Harlem; Gaynella's husband Charles Greenlee dies; Van Der Dee and Gaynella marry.

1917 The United States enters World War I; Van Der Zee's studio business thrives.

1918 End of World War I; Harlem Renaissance begins.

1920s Van Der Zee develops a signature style of portraiture and photo retouching; photographs Harlem celebrities and residents, church and social organizations, and parades and funerals.

1924 Becomes the official photographer of Marcus Garvey's Universal Negro Improvement Association (UNIA).

1927 Rachel Van Der Zee dies at age nineteen.

1928 Guarantee Photo Studio becomes G.G.G. Photo Studio, Inc.

1931 Susan Van Der Zee, Van Der Zee's mother, dies.

1943 G.G.G. Photo Studio moves to brownstone apartment in 272 Lenox Avenue; the Van Der Zees begin renting out their extra rooms.

1945 Gaynella takes out a mortgage to purchase their building; Van Der Zee takes on side work like passport photos and photo restoration to bring in extra income.

1963 Unable to pay their mortgage, their building is seized by landlord; Van Der Zees are allowed to stay and operate their studio.

1967 Reginald McGhee, director of photographic research at the Metropolitan Museum of Art, "discovers" Van Der Zee's work.

1969 Exhibition *Harlem On My Mind* opens at the Met; Van Der Zee is the single largest contributor to the show; the Van Der Zees are evicted from their home; Gaynella is hospitalized and her mental health begins to deteriorate; Van Der Zee and Gaynella find a smaller apartment on the Upper West Side of Manhattan; Charles Inniss and Reginald McGhee form the James Van Der Zee Institute; the book *The World of James Van Der Zee: A Visual Record of Black Americans* is published by Grove Press.

1975 The Friends of James Van Der Zee is formed to help the artist manage his bills and look into Van Der Zee's eviction; Donna Mussenden and James Van Der Zee meet.

1976 Gaynella dies; Van Der Zee begins collaborations with artist Camille Billops and poet Owen Dodson on *The Harlem Book of the Dead*; Billops organizes Van Der Zee's first formal portraits since 1969 as a fundraiser for Van Der Zee; Van Der Zee receives an honorary doctorate from Seton Hall University.

1978 The Met struggles with institute director Reginald McGhee and evicts the institute from its premises; the James Van Der Zee Institute dissolves and transfers its holdings to the Studio Museum in Harlem without Van Der Zee's approval; Van Der Zee marries Donna Mussenden; President Jimmy Carter awards Van Der Zee the President's Living Legacy Award.

1980 Photographs another series of portraits. Sitters include Bill Cosby, Miles Davis, Muhammad Ali, and Jean-Michel Basquiat.

1979 Jim Haskins's *The Picture Takin' Man* is published.

1983 Receives an honorary doctorate from Howard University; Dies on May 15.

1984 New York City Mayor Ed Koch declares it James Van Der Zee Week; an exhibition is mounted at the Museum of Cultural Affairs, New York, displaying his artwork and personal memorabilia, including his studio posing chair, side table, and vase; legal battle with the Studio Museum in Harlem concludes, returning 75 percent of the Van Der Zee collection back to his estate.

1993 The National Portrait Gallery in Washington, DC, organizes a retrospective of the artist's work entitled *James Van Der Zee: Photographer 1886–1983*. A book by the same title is also published.

2001 The Studio Museum in Harlem begins its annual residency program for high school students called Expanding the Walls. Students create their own work, drawing inspiration from the Van Der Zee archives at the museum.

2002 US Postal Service issues 37-cent stamps depicting Van Der Zee's portrait *My Corsage* as a part of the Masters of Photography collection.

2003 A new book, *James Van Der Zee 55* by Kobena Mercer, is published.

BOOKS

The World of James Van Der Zee: A Visual Record of Black Americans (1969)

James VanDerZee (1973)

Harlem Book of the Dead (1976)

The Harlem Book of the Dead: Photographs by James VanDerZee (1978)

A Century of Black Photographers: 1840–1960 (1983)

Black Photographers, 1840–1940: An Illustrated Bio-Bibliography (1985)

Harlem Renaissance: Art of Black America (1987)

Roots in Harlem: Photographs by James VanDerZee, from the Collection of Reginia A. Perry (1989)

James VanDerZee: The Picture-Takin' Man (1991)

VanDerZee Photographer 1886–1983 (1993)

James VanDerZee 55 Photographs (2003)

WELL-KNOWN PHOTOGRAPHS

Kate and Rachel, c.1908

Cousin Susan Porter, c. 1915

Nude by Fireplace, 1923

Identical Twins, 1924

Marcus Garvey in Regalia, 1924

Abyssininan Baptist Church, 1925

Daydreams, 1925

Alpha Phi Alpha Basketball Team, 1926

Beau of the Ball, 1926

Future Expectations, 1926

Moorish Jews, 1926

Wedding Day, 1926

Dance Class, 1928

Barefoot Prophet, 1929

Couple in Raccoon Coats, 1932

The Bride, 1937

Jean-Michel Basquiat, 1982

GLOSSARY

anti-Semitism A prejudice against, hatred of, or discrimination against Jews as an ethnic, religious, or racial group.

Black Nationalism A movement that advocates unity and self-determination for people of African descent.

bourgeois A person of, or with the characteristic of, the middle class. Typically with reference to its perceived materialistic values or conventional attitudes.

burn To increase a photo's exposure and make areas of the photo darker.

charlatan A person falsely claiming to have a special knowledge or skill; a fraud.

Civil Rights Act of 1964 A landmark piece of civil rights legislation in the United States that outlawed discrimination based on race, color, religion, sex, or national origin.

dodge To decrease a photo's exposure and make areas of the photo lighter.

double exposure The superimposition of two or more exposures to create a single image.

dry plate An early type of photographic plate made from glass treated with silver gelatin emulsion.

folk art Artwork produced by indigenous people, tradesmen, or otherwise people who are not "fine artists." The work is often utilitarian or decorative. The skills necessary are often passed down through generations or learned through apprenticeship.

Great Migration A movement of six million African Americans out of the rural Southern United States to the urban Northeast, Midwest, and West that occurred between 1910 and 1970.

hand-coloring Any method of manually adding color to a black-and-white photograph, generally either to heighten the realism of the photograph or for artistic purposes.

Harlem Riot of 1964 A series of devastating race-related riots that ripped through American cities between 1964 and 1965. In New York riots lasted six days and affected the neighborhoods of Harlem and Bed-Stuy.

ISO Or film speed, is the measurement of a photographic film's sensitivity to light.

naïve and primitive art A classification for artwork that appears childlike and simplistic in its subject matter and technique. Primitive is used to characterize art that resembles indigenous or folk art. Both terms have negative connotations because of their Eurocentric assessment of quality.

New Negro A term popularized during the Harlem Renaissance to imply a more outspoken, confident, and assertive identity for African Americans. Coined by writer and philosopher Alain LeRoy Locke.

Pan-Africanism A belief that African peoples, both on the continent and in the diaspora, share a common history and destiny.

photomontage The process and the result of making a composite photograph by cutting, gluing, rearranging, or overlapping two or more photographs into a new image.

Pictorialism An international style and aesthetic movement that dominated photography during the later nineteenth and early twentieth centuries.

postmodernism A late-twentieth-century mode of thinking that encourages skepticism toward assumed or preconceived ideas. Often used to deconstruct and question cultural, artistic, and historical notions that have been deemed by the mass culture as normal, standard, or morally correct.

pre-visualization When a photographer can plan and imagine the final print before the image has been captured.

sexton A person who looks after a church and churchyard, sometimes acting as bell-ringer and formerly as a gravedigger.

Spirit photography A type of photography whose primary attempt is to capture images of ghosts and other spiritual entities.

Spiritualism A belief that spirits of the dead have both the ability and the inclination to communicate with the living.

Universal Negro Improvement Association (UNIA) A black nationalist fraternal organization founded by Marcus Mosiah Garvey.

value An element in art that refers to the lightness or darkness of a color.

visionary art Artwork produced by self-taught individuals, usually without formal training, whose works arise from an innate personal vision that revels foremost in the creative act itself.

BOOKS

Haskins, Jim. *James Van Der Zee: The Picture Takin' Man.* Trenton, NJ: Africa World Press, Inc., 1991.

Thaggert, Miriam. *Images of Black Modernism: Verbal and Visual Strategies of the Harlem Renaissance.* Amherst, MA: University of Massachusetts Press, 2010.

Van Der Zee, James. *The World of James Van Der Zee: A Visual Record of Black Americans.* Edited by Reginald McGhee. New York: Grove Press, 1969.

Van Der Zee, James, Owen Dodgeson, and Camille Billops. *The Harlem Book of the Dead.* New York: Morgan & Morgan, 1978.

Westerbeck, Colin, ed. *The James Van Der Zee Studio.* Chicago: The Art Institute of Chicago, 2003.

Willis, Deborah. *Reflections in Black: A History of Black Photographers 1840 to the Present.* New York: W. W. Norton & Company, 2000.

WEBSITES

Death in Harlem: James Van Der Zee's Funerary Portraits

www.time.com/3807384/death-in-harlem-james-vanderzees-funerary-portraits

This article produced for *Time* magazine's photojournalism section Lightbox discusses Van Der Zee's funeral photographs and includes a photo slideshow.

Metropolitan Museum of Art Collections

www.metmuseum.org/collection/the-collection-online

Search the online collection for more information on the seventy-seven Van Der Zee prints that are part of the museum's permanent collection.

New York Times

www.newyorktimes.com

This website's archives stretch back to the periodical's beginnings in 1851. This is an incredible resource to learn more about James Van Der Zee, Harlem, and black photographers.

The Studio Museum in Harlem

www.studiomuseum.org

Visit for information about the Expanding the Walls residency and other Van Der Zee–inspired workshops and events.

The Van Der Zee Estate

www.jamesvanderzeephotographyestate.com

This Estate website is the only legitimate source for obtaining reproduction/licensing rights, photographs for exhibition, purchasting Ltd. Edition and vintage photographs, certifying authenticity of Van Der Zee photographs and learning more about his life and photography. Hosted by Mrs. Donna Mussenden Van Der Zee.

BIBLIOGRAPHY

American Visionary Museum. *What is Visionary Art?.* 2015. Accessed June 25, 2015. http://www.avam.org/stuff-everyone-asks/what-is-visionary-art.shtml.

Birt, Roger C. "For the Record: James VanDerZee, Marcus Garvey, and the UNIA Photographs." *Exposure* (Society for Photographic Education) 27, no. 4 (1990): 6.

Fraser, C. Gerald. "PHOTOGRAPHER SUES TO REGAIN WORKS." *New York Times*, December 29, 1981.

Gheno, Dan. "Van Der Zee's Craft of Love." *Santa Barbara News and Review*, May 5, 1978.

Glueck, Grace. "ART IN REVIEW; James VanDerZee Betye Saar." *New York Times*, October 25, 2002: 1.

Haskins, Jim. *James Van DerZee The Picture Takin' Man.* Trenton, NJ: Africa World Press, Inc., 1991.

Hubbard, Jaime. *Wedge Gallery to showcase James VanDerZee.* Toronto, May 1, 1999.

"James Van Der Zee Services Are Held at Trinity Cemetery." *New York Times*, May 21, 1983: 1.

Jefferson, Margo. "Book of The Times; Harlem's Face on Its Own Terms." *New York Times*, October 20, 1993: 3.

Madison Museum of Contemporary Art. *Turn Turn Turn.* 2014. Accessed June 25, 2015. http://www.mmoca.org/exhibitions-collection/exhibits/turn-turn-turn.

Michael Rosenfeld Gallery. *James VanDerZee September 12–November 2, 2002*. Accessed June 26, 2015. http://michaelrosenfeldart.com/exhibitions/james-vanderzee-harlem-guaranteed.

PBS. *Through a Lens Darkly: Black Photographers and the Emergence of a People*. 2014. Accessed June 26, 2015. http://www.pbs.org/independentlens/through-a-lens-darkly/film.html.

Shenon, Phillip. "VAN DER ZEE SUIT SETTLED." *New York Times*, May 31, 1984: 2.

Studio Museum Harlem, The. *Expanding the Walls*. 2001. Accessed June 25, 2015, http://www.studiomuseum.org/learn/expanding-the-walls.

Thaggert, Miriam. *Images of Black Modernism: verbal and visual strategies of the Harlem Renaissance*. Amherst, MA: University of Massachusetts Press, 2010.

Van Der Zee, James. *The World of James Van Der Zee: A Visual Record of Black Americans*. Edited by Reginald McGhee. New York: Grove Press, 1969.

Van Der Zee, James, Owen Dodson, and Camille Billops. *The Harlem Book of the Dead*. New York: Morgan & Morgan, 1978.

Westerbeck, Colin, ed. *The James Van Der Zee Studio*. Chicago: The Art Institute of Chicago, 2003.

Willis, Deborah. *Reflections in Black: A History of Black Photographers 1840 to the Present*. New York: W.W. Norton & Company, 2000.

Zimmer, William. "ART; Decades of Life in Harlem As Recorded by VanDerZee." *New York Times*, March 15, 1998: 3.

INDEX

Page numbers in **boldface** are illustrations. Entries in **boldface** are glossary terms.

Lara Antal is a born-and-raised Wisconsinite. She writes about art to try and understand it. She makes her own art to understand everything else.